IT ALL
MATTERS
TO
JESUS

IT ALL MATTERS TO JESUS

PRAYERS FOR BOYS

GLENN HASCALL

BARBOUR **kidz**

A Division of Barbour Publishing

Published by Barbour Publishing, Inc., 1810 Barbour Drive, Uhrichsville, Ohio 44683, www.barbourbooks.com

Our mission is to inspire the world with the life-changing message of the Bible.

 Member of the
Evangelical Christian
Publishers Association

Printed in China.

001437 0123 HA

EVERY. SINGLE. ONE. OF. YOUR. PRAYERS.

From the big to the small,
Jesus cares about them all!

God cares, cares right down to the last detail.
JAMES 5:11 MSG

Do you ever wonder if Jesus really cares about what you say to Him when you pray?

- When you ask Him to help you get a good grade in school. . .
- When you tell Him you're sad because your team lost the big game. . .
- When you share about your bad day. . .
- When you ask Him for a miracle. . .
- When you tell Him, "Thanks!" . . .

He cares about it *all*!

These 180 prayers and truth-filled scriptures will reassure your young heart that Jesus is involved in and cares about the same things you care about—from the big to the small!

TRUST FIRST

"Put your trust in the Lord Jesus Christ."
ACTS 16:31

If there is something that matters more to You than anything else, Jesus, it's that boys like me trust in You. This is the right time and a good place to do something that matters most to You. So I say, "I trust You." You can help me trust more. I say that I love You. And You can teach me to love others. I say that I choose to follow You. And You choose to lead me. There's nothing I can do to make You love me more, and there's nothing I can do to make You love me less. You love me! The words of the Bible say that You always have. If I had the choice to trust You or trust something else, then I'm going with You, Jesus. Thanks for walking with me. You know where You're going. Help me trust You enough to follow in Your steps. Amen.

COME CLOSE—
BE RIGHT—FOLLOW HARD

"Be right with Him."
MATTHEW 6:33

You aren't a choice I should put off, Lord. It matters to You that I make my friendship right with You. I could hide from You. I could pretend I've never broken Your rules. I could believe it doesn't matter. But when You reach for me, I often swat Your hand away. Your reaching hand holds care and kindness, and I keep saying I don't need Your love. But You know better. That's why You invited me to come close, be right, and follow hard. I can learn the most about love when I make You the most important thing in my life and listen to You. I can do that when I read the Bible. What I learn can help me to be right with You. Help me love what You love, so I can be happy in following wherever You lead. Trying to do this alone is something I can't do. So, please keep me company. There's a lot I need to know and a lot You can teach me. Amen.

THE PARTNERSHIP

I pray that your love will grow more and more. I pray that you will have better understanding and be wise in all things.
PHILIPPIANS 1:9

I need to learn new ways to show love to people, Jesus. You can show me, and I want You to help me practice what You teach. I know You are willing to show me what to do, but I still need to understand what You say and then do the exact things I am learning from You. This is a partnership, and You get to lead. I make the choice to follow You today, and I want Your help to follow You again tomorrow. Your love for me is a love I can share, because I know what it's like. You can show me something new every single day. Give me the wisdom to understand and then remember that this kind of love is one of the best gifts I can give—because it looks the most like You. Amen.

LISTEN, LEARN, AND LIVE

I pray that you will know what is the very best. I pray that you will be true and without blame until the day Christ comes again.
PHILIPPIANS 1:10

I can know good things, Lord, but I need to know the *best*. Good isn't good enough. When I know Your best, it helps me do everything I know You want me to do. And if I can't do it on my own, would You help me? I know I will need Your help, so I don't want to waste time by not asking now. If knowing what You want is important, then help me know everything I can about You and the plan You have for me. I don't think I can pay enough attention to learn this all on my own. Help me to be the type of student who is willing to listen, learn, and live out all the things You teach. The Bible says You will come again, and I want to still be learning from You when You come, Jesus. Amen.

THE FRUITS OF RIGHT LIVING

I pray that you will be filled with the fruits of right living. These come from Jesus Christ, with honor and thanks to God.

PHILIPPIANS 1:11

I want the words I say and the things I do to please You, Jesus. I don't always get things right, and then I feel bad. My choices matter to You. So does my friendship with You. So keep me close when I mess up. Help me want to learn more from You than I can learn from my mistakes. You can take my worst moments and make them good. I would love to have more good moments than bad, but I can't do that if I don't grow the fruit of right living. Do what needs to be done to make my life a better place for Your good fruit to grow. I don't want to stand in Your way or keep You from helping me the way I need to be helped. Amen.

HE STICKS CLOSE

The Lord is near to those who have a broken heart. And He saves those who are broken in spirit.
PSALM 34:18

There are times when I feel like something deep down inside has broken, Lord. I can't fix it. I don't know how. Sometimes I just sit in my room feeling confused and really sad. Sometimes I am angry, but I'm not sure why, and I might not even know who I am angry with. It's like someone stomped on my heart and laughed after they hurt me. But my heart matters to You. Thank You for sticking close to me when I'm not good company. Thanks for caring about the things that hurt me. I've been damaged inside by words that hurt, actions that make me want to cry, and choices that make me feel like I don't matter. Thanks for coming to stay with me even when I didn't know I could ask You to. Amen.

SOMETHING AMAZING

They gave themselves to the Lord
first. Then they gave themselves to us
to be used as the Lord wanted.
2 Corinthians 8:5

You help me and show me how to help others, Lord. This is important to You. I want it to be important to me too. If I don't know what it means to be helped, then I have no idea how to do something to help someone else. If it were up to me, I would probably just be selfish and it wouldn't even matter what other people thought or if my selfishness hurt them. But it *does* matter to You—and it should matter to me too! Help me give You my heart and my choices. Do something amazing with them. Help me get rid of my selfishness. Replace the selfish space in my life with things that mean something to You, something to me, and something to others. Amen.

THINGS TO LOOK FOR

One thing I have asked from the Lord, that I will look for: that I may live in the house of the Lord all the days of my life, to look upon the beauty of the Lord, and to worship in His holy house.

PSALM 27:4

Spending time with You is pretty incredible, Jesus. Every word of the Bible helps me understand that You are strong and can help me handle every hard thing that comes up. It matters to You that I know for sure that You love me. You've *always* cared for me. When I really understand that, then I can say, "You're amazing. You do more for me than anyone else ever has." Help me see even more of the beautiful things You do. When I notice, I want to praise You. I want to give You a big thank-You. And I want to tell others about it. They need to know You're awesome too. Amen.

THE BIBLE MATTERS

*All the Holy Writings are God-given and
are made alive by Him. Man is helped when
he is taught God's Word. It shows what is
wrong. It changes the way of a man's life.
It shows him how to be right with God.*
2 Timothy 3:16

The Words of the Bible matter, Jesus. They're important. They show people like me that not only do You never lie, but also that when You make a promise, You keep it. They tell me what I should do, what I should stop doing, and what I should never start doing. When I really pay attention and realize You are doing more than just making suggestions, I will actually start doing what You said I should do. It's a lot easier just to think about what You said than to actually do it. But that's what matters to You. My life can change, but only if I let You change me and obey what You say. What You want from me is what I need to share. Amen.

MEAN PEOPLE

*"Forgive other people and other
people will forgive you."*
LUKE 6:37

People do mean things, Lord. They make choices that do not look like the choices You make. You want me to learn from You—not from mean people. What I can learn from people who make the wrong choice isn't worth my time. The best they can teach me is how I can make another wrong choice. That's help I don't need. You say I should forgive mean people. It seems pretty hard when I think about it. It seems like mean people always get away with breaking the rules, but forgiveness isn't about saying sin is all right. Forgiveness is saying that sin doesn't have to stop me from choosing kindness and love, which matters more to You. If I can do what You ask, then You say it will be easier for people to forgive me when I'm mean. I have been mean before, You know. Sometimes even on purpose. Help me remember that forgiveness isn't just for me, but for *all* people. Amen.

I'M BUSY

Do all things without arguing and talking about how you wish you did not have to do them.
PHILIPPIANS 2:14

Sometimes an adult I trust asks me to do something for them, Jesus. It's important. They are right to ask—and I know I should do what they say—but I don't always want to. Most of the time I'd rather be doing something I want to do. Sometimes I tell them that I don't want to—and that never ends well. When I'm not willing to help, I will usually be told that I need to learn more about respect and obedience. I know they're right. You ask me to do things too—things that are important to You. Help me remember this. I could tell You all about how busy I am or that there are things I had already planned to do, but obedience is important to You. Make it important to me too. I want to know that doing what You ask will never be the wrong choice, even when other choices I've made haven't been so great. Amen.

THE CONVERSATION

Never stop praying.
1 THESSALONIANS 5:17

You could ask me about some of the things I'm interested in, and I could tell You all about them, Lord. That's stuff I know. And if You ask, I would know that You really cared about those things. Or maybe it shows You care more about me. But You have asked, haven't You? The Bible tells me to pray and then just keep praying. You want to hear about how things are going with me. You want to know what's bothering me and what kinds of things I like. You want to hear that I'm interested in what others are doing and what they need most. You want to know what I know. I don't have to be perfect when I pray. I just need to tell You about the most important parts of my day, and I can ask for Your help with the things I can't figure out on my own. The words I read in the Bible will tell me all about You. Amen.

THE MOST IMPORTANT RULE

*Love does not give up. Love is kind. Love
is not jealous. Love does not put itself up
as being important. Love has no pride.*
1 Corinthians 13:4

Love is one of the most important things to You,
Lord. I've heard that it's Your most important
rule, and I believe it. After all, You love me—and
I'm not always lovable. You know I don't always
make the right choice, but You don't throw up
Your hands in anger and leave me to think about
things. Because You're kind, I want to be close
to You. Kindness doesn't chase me away. Help
me show kindness to others, including everyone in my family. When I start to tell people why
I'm important, help me instead to remember
how important You are. What a great reminder
that bragging isn't such a great choice after all.
You give gifts that are better than anything I
could get anywhere else. Help me love people
enough not to be upset when good things happen for them. Lord, help me love You most of
all. Amen.

KNOCK IT OFF

Love does not do the wrong thing. Love never thinks of itself. Love does not get angry. Love does not remember the suffering that comes from being hurt by someone.
1 CORINTHIANS 13:5

When I want to do the wrong thing, love says, "Knock it off!" Jesus, Your love has to do that with me sometimes, especially when I can't stop thinking about myself and what I want. There are lots of things I think I want—and they mean a lot to me. Those things can even make me forget about You and what You want—and that's not good. It's not why You created love. When I get angry because things don't go my way, I need to remember that love sometimes gives up what it thought it wanted for what someone else needed. That's what love does. And when I meet mean people who speak mean words while wearing a mean face, help me remember that they need this kind of love too. Amen.

LOVE PEOPLE ENOUGH

Love is not happy with sin.
Love is happy with the truth.
1 Corinthians 13:6

I don't ever want to hear someone say, "Wow, you are a great sinner." Lord, I don't think anyone wants to hear that. Most people I know want to be remembered for good things. You want me to be remembered for good things too. Love knows that hurting other people breaks Your rules, so love is also disappointed with sin. Love and truth are very good friends. Help me to know the difference between truth and lies, and then always make the choice to share truth. With lots of work, I can get there. Help me love other people enough that I hate what sin does to them. Sin breaks people and makes happy people sad. Sin hurts anyone who comes across it—and everyone comes across it. I want to keep a safe distance from sin. Please help me do that. Amen.

DON'T CALL "TIME OUT"

Love takes everything that comes without giving up. Love believes all things. Love hopes for all things. Love keeps on in all things.
1 CORINTHIANS 13:7

Sometimes I want to throw my hands in the air, Lord. I want to say, "I give up!" Things that happen to me seem too hard. People I know lie to me. Bad things happen, and I can't stop them. I just feel like I need to call, "Time out!" But You tell me that love keeps believing that You're good. Love knows that with You, I always have hope. The Bible tells me that You protect me. So today, I choose love. And I will keep choosing it. Would You please teach me everything I can learn about love so that I am a good friend? Let Your love keep changing my heart and keep telling my mind the truth—that love is Your best answer for people who are hurting. Amen.

PURE RELIGION

Religion that is pure and good before God the Father is to help children who have no parents and to care for women whose husbands have died who have troubles. Pure religion is also to keep yourself clean from the sinful things of the world.
JAMES 1:27

The Bible talks a lot about faith, Jesus. Having faith is when I believe You are good and can rescue me from all the big and little choices I've made that break Your rules. I can sin without any help; but if I want to stop, I'll need *Your* help. I always need You, Lord. And You'll always be here for me. You don't talk much about religion; but if I want to be religious in the way the Bible says it should be, then sin will not be a choice I want to make. I want to help other people because I love You. People are really important to You, and You want people to be important to me. You might have to adjust my thinking and help me to care more about people and stay close to You. Amen.

SHOWING UP

Let us not stay away from church meetings.
Some people are doing this all the time.
Comfort each other as you see the
day of His return coming near.
HEBREWS 10:25

Spending time with You is important, Jesus. It matters to You. The truth is, You show up even when I don't. You always have something to tell me even when I'm not paying attention. You care about me even when I forget to notice. I need to spend time with Your family, and I need to hear what You have to say to us. Thank You for reminding me that You take all the things that happen to me and make them really good—better than I thought possible. Keep reminding me that it's important to spend time with You. Encourage me to keep this closeness a normal thing. Thank You for being my friend. Thank You for wanting to meet with me. Thank You for always showing up. Amen.

HELPING ME SEE

"One thing I know. I was blind,
but now I can see."
JOHN 9:25

Before I met You, I couldn't really see, Lord—at least not the important things. I was missing a whole world when I couldn't see clearly. It mattered to You, because You wanted me to see— and I needed to know what I was missing. You said faith would help me see, and now I do. I see that there is more to my future than next week's math test. There's more to today than people who are selfish and cruel. I needed to know that there was something wonderful that lived beyond what I could see without You. When I look at the world through these new eyes, I see possibilities I never would have noticed before. You don't want me to miss out on the good things You do—good things I didn't always know about. You are doing more in this world than most people think. Thank You for helping me see. Amen.

WHERE YOU'RE TAKING ME

*I forget everything that is behind me and
look forward to that which is ahead of me.*
PHILIPPIANS 3:13

Help me use my new spiritual sight to look forward, Jesus. When I look at what's in my past,
I see things that make me sad and even mad.
Sometimes I want to go back to the things You
want me to leave behind. Not everything that
I left behind was good for me. Not much I left
behind helped me. Remembering my past reminds me of hurt I don't need to remember and
choices I wish I had never made. Every time I
look back, I either want to walk back and revisit
things You told me to leave; or it makes me think
You might not want to know someone like me.
I'm thankful that You *do* want to know me. It's
really good to know You too, Lord. Maybe that's
why You tell me to stop looking back at where
I've been. I want to give all my attention to
where You're taking me. I trust it's pretty spec-
tacular! Amen.

RETURNING WHAT I CAN

*"Love the Lord your God with all your heart
and with all your soul and with all your mind."*
MATTHEW 22:37

I matter to You, and You matter to me, Jesus. Help me take the love You give me every single day and return what I can to You. Help me use my mind to remember how good You are, my heart to feel connected to You, and my soul to obey You. I want every part of who I am to care enough about You that I'm proud to share You with others. . .and I always walk in the direction You walk. I don't want to be ashamed to tell people that You're important and that I follow where You lead. You aren't something that goes viral and then gets forgotten because something new comes along. You're Jesus, my Savior. You work in my life because I matter to You. I can tell people about You because You matter to me. Amen.

CHOSEN FIRST

We love Him because He loved us first.
1 John 4:19

I didn't love You first, Lord. I couldn't. . .because I didn't know You. But You knew me and You loved me. Thanks for making a choice I couldn't. I didn't know how. But I don't think I would have been brave enough to come to You—especially if I worried that You didn't even like me or, worse, hated me. The good news is You were kind to me, and that meant a lot. Your love is what helped me turn away from all that I was so I could get closer to the me that You knew I could be, Lord. I don't think I can love anyone the way You love me; but if You're willing to teach me, then I'm willing to try. The love You have for me is amazing, and no one has ever loved me as much as You do—and no one ever will. Thank You. Amen.

THE COMPARISON

*Watch yourself, because you
may be tempted also.*

Galatians 6:1

Getting into trouble isn't hard, Jesus. Sometimes people make choices that make You sad. It's easy for me to think that I should be proud that I don't make those kinds of choices. I could even thank You that I'm not like the person I saw making a bad choice. But if I did that, then I would be making a bad choice—a choice that would not please You. But I *do* want to please You. I disappoint myself when I break Your rules. I can't imagine how You feel, but You keep reaching out to me and showing me that kindness and love will always welcome me back. Help me to stop comparing myself with other people and thinking that somehow I am better than them. You love every single one of us! Thank You, Lord. Amen.

FIND HIS FOOTPRINTS

Then Peter began to say to Him, "We have given up everything we had and have followed You."
MARK 10:28

I'm not like Peter, Lord. He gave up everything to follow You. But the only one I know who *truly* gave up everything was You. You died so I could live. You forgave, and I was forgiven. You loved me, and I saw what a difference that made. You promised a forever home in heaven with You, and it will be ready when I get there. You invited me to walk with You, and You lead every step of the way. As I follow You, You give me everything I need for the journey. I can never give what I haven't been given, but as You share Your love, forgiveness, strength, and courage with me, I can share those gifts with others who need them too. They are just like me, and they need the same things You give me. Thank You that I can follow in Your footsteps, Jesus. Amen.

THE FRIENDSHIP ROPE

One man is able to have power over him who is alone, but two can stand against him. It is not easy to break a rope made of three strings.
ECCLESIASTES 4:12

You created friends, Lord. You knew what You were doing, because there's never been a better friend than You. When I walk without You, I'm just like a piece of string that is pulled at both ends. I feel like I could snap at any time—and I have. But You send friends who can walk with me and encourage me. Because You walk with us too, our weak strings are braided with Yours to become a strong rope. You hold us together and give us strength we don't have on our own. Keep making me and my friends strong; because the only way we can do anything really worthwhile is when You—our very best friend—help us. Amen.

AMAZING

God showed His love to us. While we
were still sinners, Christ died for us.
ROMANS 5:8

Jesus, You're amazing. You don't need me to remind You; but when I say the words, it helps me remember. And I'll probably need to say it again, because I need good reminders. You gave me an even *better* reminder. The Bible is filled with so many things that show me over and over again how incredible You are. When my choices looked nothing like Yours, You reminded me that they could. And then You stepped up to show me how, helped me learn, and encouraged me to keep paying attention. The only way any of that could happen is because You did what I can't. You paid for my sins with Your life. And You did that for me before I ever broke Your rules. You didn't wait to see *if* I would make the wrong choice—You just made the right choice. Your love is amazing! Jesus, *You* are amazing! Amen.

OUT OF CONTROL

*He who is slow to anger is better than the
powerful. And he who rules his spirit
is better than he who takes a city.*
PROVERBS 16:32

My temper matters to You, Lord Jesus. When I get mad at someone, they stop listening to me. They want to be somewhere other than where I am. They don't really want to talk to me, and they probably wonder if the things they might say would help or would just make me angrier. Please help me control my temper. I want You to win the fight over the strong emotions I feel. Emotions are important, but it's not good or helpful when they stand up and push other people around. You and I need to talk more, and I need to allow You to help me. People need to see what You do to help when things look like they're getting out of control. Amen.

STICKY NOTES OF THE HEART

Your Word have I hid in my heart,
that I may not sin against You.
PSALM 119:11

I have lots of compartments in my heart, Lord, where I can hide things. I've been known to store up unkind thoughts in my heart that I bring out to think over now and then. Gossip drops in from time to time. The names and faces of mean people are posted to the walls of my heart so I remember not to like them anymore. But that's not what's supposed to be there. You say I am supposed to take the words that I read in the Bible and put them everywhere inside my heart. Let Your words be like sticky notes that I place all over inside me as reminders to make good choices. Your instructions are so very important! Amen.

MAKING TIME COUNT

*Be wise in the way you live around those who
are not Christians. Make good use of your time.
Speak with them in such a way they will want to
listen to you. Do not let your talk sound foolish.
Know how to give the right answer to anyone.*
COLOSSIANS 4:5–6

I find time for playing games and sports with
friends, Jesus. I find time to eat, sleep, and eat
some more. If I *really* want to do something, I
make the time to do it. But I take my time getting around to doing other things I need to do.
You say that time matters and I should use the
time You give me in a good way. That includes
taking time for others and telling them about
You. I can spend time talking about You when I
really want to. Help me to want to share everything about You, Lord. Help me know what to
say and how to say it. Amen.

THE GOOD ANSWER

I did not give up waiting for the Lord.
And He turned to me and heard my cry.
PSALM 40:1

When I need help, sometimes it seems like You're not around, Jesus. I know You promised never to leave me and never to pretend that You don't know me, but You don't always give me an answer as quickly as I want. If I want some chicken nuggets, they're pretty easy to get, and I don't have to wait very long. If I need something to drink, there's usually something around to drink. If I need a clean pair of socks, there's a drawer full of them. But when I pray, sometimes the answer doesn't show up right away. Am I doing something wrong? My prayer is important to You—I know that. Help me to be patient while You work things out, even when I'm not sure how You're doing it. Help me to keep watching for Your answer. I don't want to give up after You've heard my prayer. Amen.

HE SEES ME

Your eyes saw me before I was put together.
And all the days of my life were written in
Your book before any of them came to be.
PSALM 139:16

You didn't want me to wonder if You loved me, or how much, Lord. You told me in the Bible—*more than once*—that my life matters to You. You don't have to wonder what I will be one day, because You know that already, just like You knew that I would be me before I was even born. You knew my name before I was given a name. You have a plan for what You want me to be. I don't want to stop You from helping me become that man. I don't want to stop You from helping me right now. I don't need to wait, Lord. Your plans are good in the future, but they're good right now too. I matter so much to You that You don't wait to help me. I don't even have to grow up first. Amen.

SAFE STEPS

*Your Word is a lamp to my feet
and a light to my path.*
PSALM 119:105

I don't understand everything, Jesus. Maybe that's why You thought it was important to tell me that You would help me understand where to go and what to do at just the right time. The Bible is like a flashlight when it's dark and I can't see where to go next. It helps me see anything I need to avoid that might make my next step dangerous. I can be brave when I take that next step, because You help me see just enough to walk with You. Sometimes You give me only enough light to take just the next step, because You want me to trust You to lead me. If I had Your full plan from the beginning, I might think I could carry it out all on my own without Your help. Help me always to pay attention to Your directions and walk in Your good steps. Amen.

INCLUDED IN HIS PLANS

Watch and keep awake! Stand true to the
Lord. Keep on acting like men and be strong.
1 CORINTHIANS 16:13

I can get pretty sleepy, Lord. If things don't seem exciting enough, I might lose interest and even fall asleep. My courage matters to You. I need to shake off the things that distract me and pay attention to what You want me to do. My plans are not as important as Yours; and even when I don't include You in my plans, You always include me in Yours. That makes Your plans better than mine. I just need to be willing to accept Your offer to include me in Your plan and then stand strong and stay alert. I may not know what I'll be doing next, but You do! And You promise to show me at just the right time. I will need patience. Help me grow up to be brave—because even when I don't feel strong, I am still part of the plans that You have for me. Amen.

DON'T TRUST BAD THINGS

Be strong. Be strong in heart,
all you who hope in the Lord.
PSALM 31:24

I sometimes get scared when I think too much about bad things happening around me, Lord. Not just in the news I see or hear, but in things that happen to friends, family, and neighbors. It's easy to go to my room, shut the door, and hope the bad things I know are out there don't come knocking. I don't want to see them. But when I hope in You, I can look at all those things that would usually frighten me and say, "None of you is bigger than my Jesus!" Remind me of how You have always taken care of me in the past, so that I will put my hope in You for the future. Nothing is too hard for You, Lord! Amen.

NEED STRENGTH TODAY

I receive joy when I am weak. I receive joy when people talk against me and make it hard for me and try to hurt me and make trouble for me. I receive joy when all these things come to me because of Christ. For when I am weak, then I am strong.

2 CORINTHIANS 12:10

Mean people say one thing, but You say something else, Lord. When people lie, You tell the truth. When I hear words that are meant to hurt me, please help me remember who I am. I could be what they say, but I am absolutely God's child; or they could be wrong, but I am *still* God's child. No words can change that. Their meanness doesn't have to make me mean in return. Maybe they just need to know You so they can find some of the joy You have given me. I know I'm weak, but You're strong. I know I can ask for strength whenever I need it. I need it again today, Lord. Amen.

YOU DON'T CHANGE

God's plan looked foolish to men, but it is
wiser than the best plans of men. God's
plan which may look weak is stronger
than the strongest plans of men.
1 CORINTHIANS 1:25

You don't care about being popular, Lord. That's a hard game to play, and people can lose their popularity at any time. You are You, and You don't change. Because You want me to become the me that I was created me to be, I will need to change. I will need to become more like You! If I only work on becoming more popular, I'll miss out on learning to become me. Help me be real and not someone who chooses a different tone of voice depending on who I'm around. I want to change for You, Lord. I don't want to change for anyone else. If the way You do things seems foolish to some people, then I'm okay with looking a little foolish. Your plan includes promises that are never broken and a future at home with You. . .and that's more than enough for me, Jesus! Amen.

LESS TIME FOR FOOLISHNESS

God has chosen what the world calls foolish to shame the wise. He has chosen what the world calls weak to shame what is strong.
1 Corinthians 1:27

Some people think following You is foolish, Jesus. But You keep doing the things that only You can do, and those people will feel ashamed someday. They treat You badly, but Your love means You will keep reaching out to them. People think they're pretty smart when they say You are foolish; and even though they are wrong, there will come a time when they see that You matter and are worth listening to. Please take me in all my weakness and use what I have learned to share You with people who need to know You. The people who say they're strong will never be strong without You. They are lying to themselves, and other people might believe their lie. But You are the truth, and that's more important. If I pay attention to You and what You want me to do, I will have less time to pay attention to foolishness. Amen.

EVERY DECISION

"Have I not told you? Be strong and have strength of heart! Do not be afraid or lose faith. For the Lord your God is with you anywhere you go."

JOSHUA 1:9

I can say, "I will choose You, Jesus." But the truth is, there are times when I don't. I will do what I want to do and go where I want to go, and I won't check in to see if that's where my next step is supposed to go. When I do that, I will be wrong—and it will be fear that keeps me from asking for Your help when I get off track. You are my Savior, and You go with me everywhere—even when I think I am walking away. I can't do anything You don't know about, but You would still rather make me strong than see me stay weak. Help me to keep trusting You and refusing to doubt that You can *and will* help me with every step, every thought, and every choice I make. Amen.

BECAUSE THEY ASKED

Children, as Christians, obey your parents. This is the right thing to do. Respect your father and mother. This is the first Law given that had a promise. The promise is this: If you respect your father and mother, you will live a long time and your life will be full of many good things.

EPHESIANS 6:1–3

Obedience is hard, Lord. It means I have to agree to do something I might not want to do. It means I have to believe that someone else has more wisdom than I have. It means I have to respect others enough to do what they ask, just because they asked. Sometimes it's hard to give up what I'd rather be doing so I can do what someone else wants. Maybe I'd rather be playing a video game, but obedience means I put away dishes or take out the trash instead. Maybe I'd rather hang out with someone I shouldn't; but instead I go home by myself, because I know it's what You want me to do. You say obedience brings good things, so I will wait for those good things. Because obedience matters to You, please help me to be obedient. Amen.

HARD LESSONS

Troubles help us learn not to give up.
When we have learned not to give up, it
shows we have stood the test. When we
have stood the test, it gives us hope.
ROMANS 5:3–4

I want to stop thinking that if things get too hard I should stop trying, Jesus. Quitting can be as easy as breathing. But You can use any trouble I face to teach me something new. Lessons meant to last a lifetime can be hard. If learning something is easy, then it's also easy to forget. If it's easy to forget, then I will probably need to learn it again sometime. Giving up before I've learned my lesson just means I will take the test again and again until I do learn. And learning to make good choices means more happy endings. Thank You, Jesus. Amen.

WHAT OTHER PEOPLE WANT TO DO

Do not always be thinking about your own plans only. Be happy to know what other people are doing.

PHILIPPIANS 2:4

Have I told You about all the things I want to do, Lord Jesus? I probably have. I know You're interested in my plans; but I also know You're interested in the plans everyone else has too. Thinking about only the things that are important to me is selfish. You want me to pay attention to the plans and dreams of others too, things they are excited about and want to share with me. I get excited when I tell You about the things I think I would like to do, even if I might change my mind later. Still, You listen to each new plan. Help me to do that for others too. Amen.

THAT KIND OF FRIEND

My children, let us not love with
words or in talk only. Let us love
by what we do and in truth.
1 John 3:18

You want me to talk about things that are important to me, Jesus. Some things are easier to talk about than others. If I like video games, I could talk about them all day. But talking about You can be a little harder. That's especially true if I'm talking to someone who I think doesn't like You. Love tells people about You, so I need to do it! Help me to be concerned about the things that concern others and find a way to *show* and *tell* them that You care. Teach me to *show* others I care about them instead of just saying the words. People are used to trying to figure things out on their own, but to have someone step up and help is unexpected. They might want to know why I'm helping, and that would make it easier to talk about You. I want to be that kind of friend to them—and to You. Amen.

DON'T PLAY KEEP-AWAY

What if a Christian does not have clothes or food? And one of you says to him, "Goodbye, keep yourself warm and eat well." But if you do not give him what he needs, how does that help him?
JAMES 2:15–16

I'm tired of playing keep-away, Jesus. I've played it before, and I'll probably play it again. People want to know You, and I keep away from them because I don't want to talk about You. I should, but I might say the wrong thing, think I don't know enough, or be embarrassed. I play keep-away even when I know people need help. I can say some nice things but refuse to help. That kind of choice doesn't help anyone—it just makes people think I don't care. Maybe they think You don't care either. If I can do something to help someone, I don't want to take too much time to think about it. I just want to be willing to help—like You help me. Amen.

THE WAY YOU SEE THEM

Nothing should be done because of pride or thinking about yourself. Think of other people as more important than yourself.

PHILIPPIANS 2:3

Lord Jesus, You want me to see other people and what they need as more important than me and my needs. Most people think they need to make themselves happy first and only be concerned about the things that interest them. This doesn't mean they aren't important; it just means they aren't the only ones who are important. If I can remember how important other people are to You, then maybe I can begin to see them the way You see them. Help me to stop thinking I'm the only person who is special to You by remembering that there is no one who *is not* special to You. You love everyone. And You ask me to make other people feel special too. That's what You do for me. Thank You! Amen.

THOUGHTS WORTH THINKING

Think as Christ Jesus thought. Jesus has always been as God is. But He did not hold to His rights as God. He put aside everything that belonged to Him and made Himself the same as a servant. . . . He became human by being born as a man.

PHILIPPIANS 2:5–7

Your thoughts are worth thinking, Lord. You thought them first—and now I can think them too. I can learn from the lessons in the Bible, and I can think Christlike thoughts when the Holy Spirit teaches me. You thought enough of every human who has ever lived to come to earth in a human body. When You did that, You put Your rights as God on the shelf. Together You created everything, but human beings treated You very badly. You became a servant to those who were created. Those are thoughts worth thinking, because they mean You thought more of me than You thought of Yourself. And I am so thankful. Amen.

A GOOD DISCOVERY

*"The Lord is God. There is
no other except Him."*
DEUTERONOMY 4:35

Every day it seems like there's something new to discover, Jesus. It's often something with buttons and a screen, but it could be a toy or a new book. The things I can own seem to be getting better all the time—and many will make it to my Christmas wish list—but I might change my mind next week, because there will probably be something even newer to discover. But You mean more than any of the things I *think* I need. What I've always needed is You. There is nothing more awesome than You. No one can match You in any way. I don't ever need to change my mind about You. You are worth knowing today, and I won't need to change my mind next week. We celebrate Christmas because You were the greatest gift ever given, and You're on my wish list. I don't want anything to impress me more than You do, Lord. Amen.

GENTLE WISDOM

Who among you is wise and understands?
Let that one show from a good life by the
things he does that he is wise and gentle.
JAMES 3:13

I can be smart and still not understand You, Lord. If I do start to understand You, then I'm learning to be wise—and that's not the same thing as being smart. If I know everything I need to know to put a computer together, then I might be smart. If I know how to use the computer and not let it become more important than You are, then I might be showing some wisdom. It matters to You that I become wise enough to make good choices and show the same kindness You show to me. I don't want people to be impressed just because I know a lot of facts. I want them to be impressed by You, because You show up in the things I say and do. I would be happy to trade being smart for being wise. Can I trade today? Amen.

STAY WITH JESUS

*Get wisdom and understanding. Do not forget
or turn away from the words of my mouth.*
PROVERBS 4:5

You don't want me to act as if I don't know what You want, Lord, especially when I really do know. When I do something like that, I am not being wise and it proves that I don't really understand You very well. The Bible gives rules for how to live my life in a way that pleases You and introduces other people to You. I can't act as if what it says doesn't matter. I can't stay with You and turn away from You at the same time. That's like cheering and booing for my favorite sports team at the same time. I am either for You or against You—and I want to be *for* You. Please help me pay attention to the words in the Bible. Help me to understand what they mean and to do what You want me to do. Amen.

REFORMED ACTOR

Do not act like the sinful people of the world. Let God change your life. First of all, let Him give you a new mind. Then you will know what God wants you to do. And the things you do will be good and pleasing and perfect.
ROMANS 12:2

I'm a good actor, Lord Jesus. I deserve an award, but I don't want it. Any memory of my acting skills just makes me sad. I act like You don't matter, like the Bible doesn't matter, and like I can do whatever I want and it's no big deal. I'm so good at acting that people believe me—and they are believing a lie. And even though other people can also be really good actors, You want me to stop. You want me to make changes that let people see what's real and get rid of the act. Change my mind about what's important. You have things I could be doing that don't require any acting skill, because they are real and are pleasing to You. Amen.

STOP AND GO

Even if I am free to do all things, I will not do them if I think it would be hard for me to stop when I know I should.
1 CORINTHIANS 6:12

You tell me "no" a lot less than people think, Lord. There are all kinds of things I can do that never break Your rules, but I don't want any of those things to come between You and me. Everyone follows someone, and I want to follow You. I don't want to be sidetracked by following someone who sings, plays games, or just seems more interesting. I don't want to realize I've gone too far when You need me to stop and re-member You. I get to follow You because I want to, and You let me. I want to go where You go. I want to do what the most important person I will ever know asks me to do. I want to keep talking to You, Jesus. Amen.

THE TRUSTING POINT

*Trust in the Lord with all your heart, and do
not trust in your own understanding.
Agree with Him in all your ways, and
He will make your paths straight.*
PROVERBS 3:5–6

Can I trust myself, Lord? Am I as dependable as You are? Do I really understand as much as You do? I know You are trustworthy and worth following. I don't know why I stop to think about whether I should do what You want. You have good reasons for everything You do, even when I don't know what they are. Sometimes I just need to follow so I can learn and understand more. This is important, because I will learn from the things I do. I would rather learn from making good choices than from making mistakes that make You sad. Help me quickly see that Your way is best and that You always lead in a good direction—to a really good place. What's the point of trusting myself when I don't know what I'm doing? This is why I follow You, Jesus. Amen.

MORE THAN ENOUGH

"The Lord is the One Who goes before you.
He will be with you. He will be faithful
to you and will not leave you alone.
Do not be afraid or troubled."
DEUTERONOMY 31:8

Sometimes I feel lonely in the middle of the night, Jesus. I also feel alone in places where there are a lot of people but no one seems to know I exist. Maybe I've just forgotten to look for You. You didn't leave me—not even once. You created the path I need to follow, and You keep showing me each next step. Paying attention is what I need to do. I know I can always talk to You, but I don't always listen very well—and You never yell to get my attention. Help me tune out the noise that makes it hard to hear You. Then when You speak, encourage me to obey. Take my anxiety and toss my fear in the trash. I don't need either one, because I have You—and You are more than enough! Amen.

MORE VALUABLE THAN MONEY

Keep your lives free from the love of money.
Be happy with what you have. God has said,
"I will never leave you or let you be alone."
HEBREWS 13:5

What I do with money matters to You, Lord Jesus. You don't tell me that I shouldn't have money. You tell me to make sure that money doesn't become so important that I can't find time to spend with You. You want me to be happy with what I already have. I should remember that if it weren't for You, I'd have nothing. Your friendship helps me through hard days, helps me understand that You want to help me, and reminds me that You aren't going anywhere. No matter where I go, You come with me. You see me when I obey, and You see me when I break Your rules. Even then, You still choose never to leave me feeling lonely. Help me see You as more valuable than money, because no matter what happens, I have You. Amen.

WHAT YOU CAN'T CONTROL

*Why are you sad, O my soul? Why have you
become troubled within me? Hope in God,
for I will praise Him again for His help
of being near me. O my God, my soul is
troubled within me. So I remember You.*
PSALM 42:5–6

Good days are amazing, but bad days are normal, Lord. On bad days, I have a choice to make: I can think of how hard they are and wonder why I have to go through another hard day, or I can pay attention to You, ask for Your help, and stand by to see what You will do with this troubled day. I don't know why I spend so much time on things I can't control when I can ask You to control the uncontrollable, make the impossible possible, and calm the battle taking place in my mind and heart. I want to remember I don't need to be sad when trouble comes—I just need to remember who You are, because nothing stands up to You and wins. Amen.

EVERYTHING WILL BE FINE

This hope is a safe anchor for our souls. It will never move. This hope goes into the Holiest Place of All behind the curtain of heaven.
HEBREWS 6:19

If I am a big boat, then let me reach for Your big hope, Jesus. The Bible calls hope an "anchor." When the waves smash into the side of my life, help me use hope to keep me from falling apart. Hope holds me in place, because You hold the anchor and make sure that even when things are the most difficult, You bring possibility to my problems. Your hope helps me trust that at the end of the storm, everything will still be all right and I will still have hope. You could just say the word and my difficulty would be over, but maybe You're just waiting for me to look the storm in the face and say, "My Jesus is with me, and everything is going to be fine." Help me use this hope to trust You even more. Amen.

GUILTY

"I always try to live so my own heart tells me I am not guilty before God or man."
ACTS 24:16

When I break Your rules, I'm guilty, Lord. I know it. You do too. I want to be perfect, but humans aren't perfect. You don't want me to give up. I'll fail and You'll forgive. I'll need help and You'll help me. I'll stumble and You'll catch me. You want me to make choices that say I'm not guilty. I don't have to be guilty before You, because You forgive me when I fail and help me choose something better than I have chosen before. I'm thankful that You can help me succeed. I need Your help when my choices are less than my best, Lord. That means I'll need Your help every day of my life. Amen.

JUST WHAT I NEED

A God-like life gives us much when we are happy for what we have. We came into this world with nothing. For sure, when we die, we will take nothing with us.
1 Timothy 6:6–7

When I was born, I was given clothes because I didn't have any, Lord. I was given a place to live and some toys, because I couldn't earn money. As I began to grow up, You gave me hope when I lived in fear, faith when I struggled to believe, and love when I was alone. I'm here because You made me, and nothing I can do on my own will ever be as impressive. I arrived as a baby with nothing. When my life is over, I will leave this world with nothing—and You will *still* be taking care of me. There are lots of things I say are mine, but most will not last forever. The only things that will last are You and the people I love and who love me. Amen.

SOMETHING BETTER THAN MONEY

A good name is to be chosen instead of many riches. Favor is better than silver and gold.
PROVERBS 22:1

It matters if people think I represent You well, Jesus. My reputation has meaning, which is why You want me to come to You for help in making good decisions. When I make choices on my own, I usually have to apologize to someone. I can hurt feelings, cause people to stop trusting me, and take things that don't belong to me. You never wanted that for me, which is why You gave me rules to follow. If I really love people the way You say I should, then I won't do things that hurt them or make them stop trusting me. All the money in the world won't make people trust me more. You always keep Your promises; help me keep more of mine. I don't want to promise more than I can do; but when I make a promise, I will need Your help to keep it. Amen.

NO SHADOWS OF DOOM

The Lord is my light and the One Who saves me.
Whom should I fear? The Lord is the strength
of my life. Of whom should I be afraid?
PSALM 27:1

Danger makes a shadow that frightens me, Lord Jesus. What seems scary also seems dark. My strength goes away at the sight of these shadows of doom. But fear doesn't have to be my response. Fright doesn't have to show up at night. You bring light, and the doom shadows disappear. Nothing is too hard for You, and that won't change. Nothing makes You afraid, and nothing ever will. You probably find it hard to see why I'm afraid, but I find it hard to believe that there's nothing to fear. I get strength from You, but I sometimes forget. You're the one who saves, and I need a reminder. There is nothing to be afraid of—You even work overnight. Thank You, Jesus. Amen.

WHEN IT'S HARD TO TRUST

For God did not give us a spirit of fear.
He gave us a spirit of power and
of love and of a good mind.
2 TIMOTHY 1:7

Fear is not from You, Lord. Fear never helps me. It doesn't want me to sleep. It won't let me make good decisions. It keeps me from trusting You. When I am afraid, nothing seems safe. But You give me strength to stand up when fear wants me to run and hide. You give me power in my spirit that knows You have my back. You give my mind something new to think about, because the Bible says over and over again, "Do not be afraid." Help me to remember that I am not alone and do not need to be afraid, because You are *always* with me. Amen.

FEELING LOW BUT RISING

Let yourself be brought low before the Lord.
Then He will lift you up and help you.
James 4:10

It matters to You that I know I sin, Lord. You say that everyone sins, so that includes me. Maybe the reason You want me to know for sure that I break Your rules is because I will also need to know for sure that I need You to save me from the choices that led me to sin in the first place. When I'm feeling sad about what I've done, I know that I need You. When I need You, I will ask for Your help. You lift me up and remind me that I'm forgiven and loved. So even when I start sad, I can end happy. I can't do that when I pretend I've done nothing wrong. I can't do that when I think I'm better than other people. I can't do that when I let pride stop me from being honest with You. Amen.

NOTICING THE GOOD

Let another man praise you,
and not your own mouth. Let a
stranger, and not your own lips.
PROVERBS 27:2

You don't want me to say, "Hey, look at me, Jesus!" I don't need to do that, because You already notice me—and You don't miss anything. You also don't want me to try to get other people to notice the good things I do. Let my words never say, "Hey, look at me!" It will always be better to let people say nice things about me instead of me saying nice things about me. But I can say nice things about them. I don't want my life to look like a billboard that tells people all about me and why I'm the best guy they could know. I want people to know the best Jesus—and You're Him. I want them to know that any good they see in me is because of You. Help me refuse to make good outcomes all about me when You work everything out in a way I never could. Amen.

SEE THE GOOD

*You who look for God, let your
heart receive new strength.*
PSALM 69:32

I want to keep my eyes open so I can notice the things You're doing, Lord. I want to tell You when I see them. There are a lot of things I miss when I stop paying attention to You. That could be why You want me to refuse to let things get in the way of what You're doing in my life. My strength matters to You because You know that if I don't come to You, I'll stay weak. Without Your strength, I'll struggle and fail. May I pay attention to You, even when I want to pay attention to other things. Give me a heart that gets stronger, a mind that gets wiser, and a spirit that's connected to You. There are things only You can teach. Because I'm easily distracted, I'll need You to be patient as I learn to follow You every step of the way. Amen.

BEYOND THE MESS

For His loving-kindness for those
who fear Him is as great as the
heavens are high above the earth.
PSALM 103:11

Life is messy, Jesus. When I think things aren't going too well and then they don't seem to get better, I feel disappointed and wonder why they can't be fixed. There must be a better way to live than what I sometimes see around me. But Your love is bigger than the mess, and Your kindness covers absolutely everything. You could destroy anyone who doesn't agree to do exactly what You say, but if You did, how could anyone survive? So I live in a mess that I might not have created, but I can know that You are in control and that You love me and will always treat me with kindness and take care of me. Thank You so much, Lord. Amen.

HE WANTS TO BE FOUND

*You, O Lord, are a God full of love
and pity. You are slow to anger and
rich in loving-kindness and truth.*
Psalm 86:15

Sometimes I want You to be in a hurry, Lord Jesus. I want You to rush into situations and make things better. I want You to fix what's broken. I want sinners to stop sinning, I want all decisions to be good, and I want people who break Your rules to stop breaking them. If You could do this today, I would be grateful. It seems like something You would want to do, but You know it's more important that people be given free will—the chance to decide how they will respond when You call them to follow and obey You. So instead of rushing to make everything good, You patiently wait for people to turn to You so they can get the help they need to make better choices. Amen.

LOYALTY

"No one can have two bosses. He will hate the one and love the other. Or he will listen to the one and work against the other. You cannot have both God and riches as your boss at the same time."
Matthew 6:24

I say I want to follow You, but then I act like things are more important, Lord. That's a problem, because You don't want anything to become more important than You. When I spend more time with things, it makes it harder for me to get to the place where You can do Your best work in my life. While it might make sense to me to say that I honor You but chase after something else, You know it won't work out. I will spend less time with You, and the more I think about other things, the less important You will be to me. This decision matters to You, because You gave Your life so I could be close to You. I don't want to turn my back on Your gift. Amen.

BE PATIENT WITH OTHERS

*Love each other with a kind heart
and with a mind that has no pride.*
1 PETER 3:8

Because You are patient with me, I need to be patient with others, Jesus. You give people who sin the chance to seek out Your forgiveness. You don't stop loving people when they sin. Your kindness is the invitation they need to learn more about You. I am happy that You've done this for me, and now You ask me to do the same for others—to love and forgive them. If I can bring Your love with me when I talk to people, then they might feel like they can share the things that bother them—things You can help them with. Let me be someone others can come to so they can learn more about Your love. Amen.

FRUIT TO SHARE

*[Jesus said,] "When you give much fruit,
My Father is honored. This shows
you are My followers."*
JOHN 15:8

Fruit can't grow on its own, Lord. Fruit grows on trees, vines, and bushes. It has to be attached to a plant with roots in order to grow. That's how fruit gets nutrition. In the same way, You want me to grow fruit by being connected to You. You say that You are the vine and Your people are the branches. For fruit to grow in my life, I have to be connected to You, the vine. I can't grow spiritual fruit without You, so forgive me when I try. People will recognize me as someone who follows You when they see my good fruit—things like love, joy, and kindness. Then they will see how good it is to follow You. I want to stay close to You, so that even more fruit can grow and I'll have more to share with people who need to experience You. Amen.

THE TROUBLE WITH LITTLE THINGS

Why do you hate your Christian brother? We will all stand before God to be judged by Him.
ROMANS 14:10

Most people think Christians always love other Christians, Lord. That is exactly what You want, but it doesn't always happen that way. Sometimes I can let little things keep me from loving someone else who follows You. I might even think that I don't really need to—maybe it's possible to leave loving other people up to You. But I am wrong when I believe that You should do it and I can just stand by and watch. It seems like You're saying that if I don't love other Christians, then I hate them. I never thought about it like that. I only thought it meant that I didn't like them very much. If my only choices are love or hate, then help me to love everyone in Your family. These are the same people who love You—the people You love. Now it's my turn, Jesus. Amen.

THE BURDEN

[Jesus said,] "Come to Me, all of you who work and have heavy loads. I will give you rest. Follow My teachings and learn from Me. I am gentle and do not have pride. You will have rest for your souls. For My way of carrying a load is easy and My load is not heavy."
MATTHEW 11:28–30

I've tried so many times to carry my own burdens, Lord Jesus. I've tried carrying them in different ways, but none have worked. Some burdens may not seem very heavy at first, but I can't carry them for very long. And You don't want me to. You want me to realize that the burdens I face are too big for me. You have offered to give me relief from my burdens. I just need to turn them over to You. Please be patient with me as I learn to trust You instead of depending on myself. Amen.

YOU WATCH ME

He who is right in his walk is sure in his steps, but he who takes the wrong way will be found out.
PROVERBS 10:9

I don't know why I would ever think that You won't miss me if I wander away, Jesus. But You do. Your eyes see me walk from progress to trouble. You're with me before I take my first step away from You, but when I take that step, Your eyes are on me. You watch me when I know the right step and take it too. When I'm heading in the right direction, You're cheering me on. You know me, and You love me. There's nothing I can do that is hidden from You. I can't hide, run away, or lie to You without You knowing. There's also nothing that's hidden when I make the right choice. I can't share Your love, shine Your light, or tell the truth about You without You knowing. Please keep my spiritual life moving in Your direction. Amen.

BAD INFORMATION

*Do not lie to each other. You have
put out of your life your old ways.*
COLOSSIANS 3:9

I've been warned, Lord. Lying to other people matters to You. You don't want me to do it. That's the way I used to do things. When You gave me a new life, there were new rules to follow and new gifts to open. One of Your impressive gifts is truth. In fact, You say You are the way, the truth, and the life. I read truth in the Bible, and You help me obey it. The old rules I lived by don't work with the new life You've given me. You never tell lies. But people in the world tell lies because they follow the devil who is the father of lies. Help me to know Your truth so that I won't fall into the trap of believing lies. Make Your truth clear to me so I know when I'm being lied to. Then I will be able to make good choices that please You. Thank You, Jesus. Amen.

THE MESSAGE

*Then Jesus said to them again, "May
you have peace. As the Father has
sent Me, I also am sending you."*
JOHN 20:21

You've given me an assignment, Jesus. And if I get all stressed out, You remind me that You sent peace first so I don't have to worry. You let me know I have Your example to follow. You came, and now You're sending me. I can follow Your example. Even when I make the choice to ignore what I'm being asked to do, You still encourage me to go. There's nothing that can stop Your message from getting out. When You ask me to take it, then You want it delivered. Your message matters, because it changes the way I do things, and it can change the way other people do things. It helps people know there is a right way to live and that Your plan makes it possible. Help me want to share this really good news, because people need to know. Amen.

TRUTH STANDS

Stand up and do not be moved. Wear a belt of truth around your body. Wear a piece of iron over your chest which is being right with God.
Ephesians 6:14

You are strong, and You make me strong, Jesus. When Your enemy the devil tries to tell me that I don't know what I'm talking about and calls You a liar, help me remember that I've been given a belt of truth as part of my armor. I can remind the enemy that You are the only one who has ever told the complete truth about everything. The devil wants me to be afraid, and fear never tells the truth about anything. Fear wants me to make bad things seem bigger and good things seem like no real help. Please keep my strength up by teaching me to believe that truth always comes from You and lies never will. Help me stand and not move until You give the word. And when I move, help me to make sure You're the leader I follow. Amen.

PROVE MY DOUBTS WRONG

Give all your worries to Him
because He cares for you.
1 PETER 5:7

I get worried. I admit it, Lord. My mind keeps thinking about the worst thing that could happen even when I remember that You take care of everything. I can choose to believe that You're in control, or I can tell You that I don't think You're big enough. When I worry, I'm saying that I don't trust You. But You're bigger than anything I face. You always prove my doubts wrong. I'm left to say that You are right and I am wrong. So help me to give You all my worries and to trust that You care and will patiently show me Your kindness as I have faith in You. Amen.

TIME TO TRY TRUST

*"Which of you can make himself
a little taller by worrying?"*
MATTHEW 6:27

Sometimes I think worry is useful, because I want it to mean that I care about other people, Lord Jesus. If worry could make people taller, I'd be living in a land of giants. If worry could add one more minute to my life, I'd probably live forever. But I'm not a giant, and worry has never added even one second to anyone's life. Since You care about everyone, then worry can't be the right way to show that I care. You know how everything turns out, and You win. You help at just the right time. So if worry is not what I should be doing, then I want to try trust instead. Trust will help me sleep better and think clearer. Trust will help me get closer to You. Nothing is too difficult for You, Jesus. Amen.

GROWING TRUST PLANTS

*Do not worry. Learn to pray about
everything. Give thanks to God as
you ask Him for what you need.*

PHILIPPIANS 4:6

You say worry is off-limits, Jesus. Please stop the
worry in my heart and mind. Worry grows like a
weed, and the roots go deep. Worry takes all the
stuff that helps make good things grow, and I
can't seem to find anything else inside my heart
but worry plants. I don't know how to stop them
from growing, and I don't know how to get rid
of them. But You tell me there is a way, and I am
actually doing it right now—I am praying to You.
You said I could pray about everything, and since
worry is something I struggle with, I'm praying
that You set me free from it. You can take my
worry, pull the roots, and allow trust plants to
grow where worry once grew wild. Amen.

THE PEACE CURE

[Jesus said,] "Peace I leave with you. My peace I give to you. I do not give peace to you as the world gives. Do not let your hearts be troubled or afraid."
JOHN 14:27

Worry can make people sick, Lord. It can bother their stomachs. They usually take medicine to help them feel better. But You have a cure that works even better—peace. The peace that You give isn't a peace that means everyone gets along; it is much more personal. Peace calms my heart and makes worry feel unwelcome. Your peace means that no matter what is happening around me, I don't feel the need to worry because You care enough to take care of things. I don't need to feel disturbed, and I don't need to be afraid. You've given me peace, and You want me to trust. These two can cure worry and allow me to see life as more of an adventure than something that makes me sick, weak, and sad. Thank You, Jesus. Amen.

THE BETTER PLACE
I NEED TO BE

I am sure that God Who began the good
work in you will keep on working in you
until the day Jesus Christ comes again.
PHILIPPIANS 1:6

Some days I wonder if I'll ever be what You need me to be, Lord. I can be stubborn. I might skip Your lessons or avoid Your tests. But the Holy Spirit keeps working to teach me things I need to know so I can do the things You want me to do. When I'm stubborn, He outlasts me. If I miss a class, He reschedules. This isn't to annoy me but to prepare me for a better way of life. You can teach me even when I don't want to cooperate, but it's always easier if I want to learn. Keep up the good work, Jesus. I want to be more like You. Amen.

DON'T STOP MY FEET

*Be at peace with all men. Live a
holy life. No one will see the Lord
without having that kind of life.*
HEBREWS 12:14

Worry stops me from seeing You, Jesus. It even
stops my feet from following You. It leaves me
alone when I need a friend. Worry can do nothing good for me. It doesn't help others. It won't
let me listen to You. It hopes I will believe lies.
It believes I've been abandoned. But I haven't.
I'm not. I never will be. I'll need to see You if I
want my life to be useful in helping other people find You. My life is like an electronic device
that's fully charged. I'm ready to be useful. I'm
ready to be put to work. You have a plan, and I'm
listening. Help me remember to see the value
in everyone I talk to. At the end of this day,
when You're recharging me to tackle tomorrow,
help me to find rest and leave anything that has
worried me in Your hands. Amen.

I AM WELCOME TO YOUR FOREVER

"For God so loved the world that He gave His only Son. Whoever puts his trust in God's Son will not be lost but will have life that lasts forever."
JOHN 3:16

You did something that no one saw coming, Lord. You astonished the world by saying, "I love everyone. No one will be left out!" No one? No one! Whenever anyone trusts You, they're safe, rescued, and forgiven. One amazing part of Your love is that once You choose me, You never reject me. You love me so much that You want me to live with You forever. This is why worry is never welcome at Your house—and it shouldn't be welcome in mine. Your love lasts forever. Your life lasts forever. You accept me forever. I have nothing to worry about. Thank You! Amen.

USING THE GIFT

*God has given each of you a gift. Use it to help
each other. This will show God's loving-favor.*
1 Peter 4:10

Everyone has something very special that You
give them to do, Lord. You have a lot of different
kinds of gifts, and You give one kind of gift to one
person and something else to another. Because
You know everything about everyone, You know
what gifts they could really use. For instance,
You give one person the gift of preaching and
another person the gift of helping others. The
point of You giving gifts to people is so that
they in turn can use them to give gifts to others.
Help me pay attention to what gift You might
want to give me. Let me pay attention to other
people who can help me understand what
You've given me. Then, once I know what that
special gift is, help me use it to be useful to You.
Amen.

HAVE YOU MET MY JESUS?

O give thanks to the Lord. Call on His name.
Make His works known among the people.
PSALM 105:1

I discovered something other people should discover, Jesus—You. No one matters more than You. I couldn't survive without You. When I pray, I call out Your name, and You're listening from the very first word I say. It doesn't even matter if it's late at night and I'm afraid of the dark—You listen. I need to tell someone about You. Give me the chance and make me bold enough to say, "Have you met my Jesus? He's awesome!" Because You do good things for me, help me use my words to let people know what You did and how it helped me. I want my trust in You to help others think more about You. I want people to know that You're famous and that there's no one else they could meet that will ever mean as much. Amen.

A WONDER SHARED

*The hearing ear and the seeing
eye were both made by the Lord.*
Proverbs 20:12

When people see, they see things only You could make, Lord Jesus. When they hear, they hear voices created by You. It's important that people see me honoring You and sharing my story about You. It matters that when I speak, people will have every reason to believe You mean something to me. Since what they see and hear from me can help them believe You're important, maybe they'll choose to listen to more good news about a good God. You made the mind to think, eye to see, and ear to hear. You made the heart to feel, hands to touch, and mouth to taste. You take every sense and allow people to experience Your goodness. This might be a tasty piece of fruit, the touch of a grandparent's hand, or good news about a good friend. Your wonder can be found everywhere, and this wonder can be shared. Amen.

MORE THAN IMPRESSED

Whatever is good and perfect comes to us from God. He is the One Who made all light. He does not change.
JAMES 1:17

I know You give good gifts, Lord, and I thank You for sending them. Help me to be wise enough to accept them, strong enough to use them, and impressed enough to tell people where these gifts came from. You don't send monthly upgrades, because You don't change and Your truth doesn't either. You're not like computer updates, because Your truth can't be hacked—and the programming was perfect from the beginning. I'm the only one who can mess things up when I think wrong thoughts about You and the things You've said. So let me see the good, share the awesome, and love the best news ever. Give me all the reminders You can that You were good yesterday, You are good today, and You will be good tomorrow. You help me see Your work and then help me feel secure knowing that You'll always be dependable and trustworthy. Amen.

BRAND-NEW ME

For if a man belongs to Christ,
he is a new person. The old life
is gone. New life has begun.
2 CORINTHIANS 5:17

My choices matter to You, Lord Jesus. The choice that will always start me on a journey with You is when I trade my past for Your future. I give up doing the things the way I used to do them, and You can teach me a new way to do things. You can make me something different and better than I was before. You help me do things I couldn't do before. You take my fear and send it away. You take my weakness and make me strong. You take my sin and tell me that I'm no longer guilty. You love me, and I'm learning to love You too. I want to keep walking with You, and I want You to keep teaching me. Living life without You was not as good as living life with You. Thank You for staying with me, helping me, and loving me. Amen.

NEW SPIRIT, NEW HEART

"I will give you a new heart and put a new spirit within you. I will take away your heart of stone and give you a heart of flesh."
Ezekiel 36:26

Lord, I want every part of me to know You. I want my mind to think about You, my feet to follow You, and my voice to speak to You. You must be glad that this is what I want, because that's what You want too. Take away all the things that make me look away from You. Help me see You, hear You, and know You. When my heart is not useful to You and I need a replacement, help me to be willing to let You change whatever You need to change to make me what I should be. I want to think enough of You that it just makes sense to let You take what I don't need—so You can give what I can't get anywhere else. Amen.

THE WORK HE DOES

We are His work. He has made us to be-long to Christ Jesus so we can work for Him. He planned that we should do this.
EPHESIANS 2:10

You want me to work for You, Jesus. If Yours is a family business, then You already have a place for me. I'm happy to be part of Your family. I can't do the right thing without You. I fail, and I will fail again. Working for You means I'm not working against You. I'm on Your side, and that's just where You want me to be. When You say I can work for You, that means I can learn to be capable, able, and willing to do something more than I can do right now. It means You believe in me, because I'm willing to learn from You. Thanks for another really great plan, Lord Jesus. Amen.

BETTER THAN CLAY PANCAKES

*O Lord, You are our Father. We are the
clay, and You are our pot maker. All
of us are the work of Your hand.*
ISAIAH 64:8

Clay can be made into anything, Jesus, and
the Bible says I am clay. Clay can be made
into lots of cool things, but my clay art mostly
looks like pancakes or worms. But in Your hands,
my life becomes something amazing. You work
my life clay until it's soft. You start to mold me
into what I should be, but sometimes I can be
hard to mold and unwilling to change. I want to
be easier to work with. The stories of impressive people who loved You began when they let
You reshape their lives and remake their futures.
I'm tired of being a pancake or worm. Do something much better with my life than I have ever
been able to do. I love watching You work in me.
Anything good that has ever been made has
been made by You. Amen.

WILLING TO WAIT
FOR WELL DONE

Whatever work you do, do it with all your heart. Do it for the Lord and not for men.
COLOSSIANS 3:23

Sometimes when I do something good, I'm okay if no one notices You, Lord. I don't mind if people think I am better than most because I did something nice, good, and memorable. But when I do my best work and make it all about me, then I'm not really doing those things for You. I should put everything I have into everything I do—and not to be noticed by anyone but You. Help me remember that I don't need a crowd to do the right thing. It's okay with me if I need to wait to hear You say, "Well done!" I want to make my best work a gift I can give to You. You've already given me more than I will ever deserve. Thank You, Jesus! Amen.

IMPORTANT THINGS

*"He that is faithful with little things
is faithful with big things also."*
LUKE 16:10

Air is not a little thing, Lord, but it can seem that way. I need air all the time, but air seems to be everywhere—so it's easy to forget that life would be impossible without it. If I think of air as a little thing, then You have always been faithful to make sure I have enough air. I believe You can be trusted with things I think about more often. There are things I think of as big. They are important to me, and You make sure every little *and* big thing I face is something You care about. Now it's my turn. You want me to be faithful to do the little things, and when I'm faithful doing things I may not even think are important, then You will trust me with bigger things. I need to believe that what You want is important so it will be important to me too. Amen.

FAITHFUL WHEN I
DIDN'T KNOW YOU

*[God said,] "I will not take my loving-kindness
from him. I will always be faithful to him.
I will not break My agreement."*
PSALM 89:33–34

When You do what You say You will do, that's called a promise. And You're the best at it, Lord. You've never made a promise that You didn't keep. Your loving-kindness is forever, and Your faithfulness never expires. I can count on You—and I do. I can pray to You—and I am. I can follow You—and I need to keep following. Thank You for showing me what it looks like to be faithful. You don't say that You'll like me as long as I like You. You say You loved me even when I didn't know You. You cared for me when I couldn't care less. You found me when I was running away. But I don't want to run anymore. I don't want to hide. I don't want to ignore Your kind and loving faithfulness. Now that I know You, I want to stay close. Amen.

JESUS IS MY FRIEND

[Jesus said,] "You are My friends
if you do what I tell you."
JOHN 15:14

I get to be Your friend, Lord. *Me!* I'm just a human boy. But God was so pleased with His creation that He didn't hide me in the corner or in a box somewhere because He didn't think I looked right, sounded right, or made the best choices. No, He sent You, Jesus, to show me that I could be Your friend—and that You would be mine. When others turn away, You stay. You can be trusted, so I'll trust You. Help me to be trustworthy. And even when I miss the mark, You won't stop being my friend. You just remind me that there are things friends do for each other. You always do those things, and I need Your reminders to help me remember what being Your friend looks like. Help me to make choices that look like being Your friend really matters to me. Amen.

NO FOOLING

Do not let anyone fool you. Bad people can make those who want to live good become bad.

1 Corinthians 15:33

If I need reminders that You're my best friend, Jesus, then I'll need to remember that not everyone is Your friend. If they aren't, then they don't want me to be Your friend either—and that matters to You. It should matter to me. They need You for a friend, because when You aren't their friend, they won't want me to make the choices You want me to make. They might even convince me that You're not worth having as a friend. I might listen when they say they think it's foolish to believe in You. That's when my choices might say that I don't want to be friends anymore—and that's a bad choice to make. I've never known someone who doesn't love You who has never let me down, was completely trustworthy, and then told me that You'll always be my best friend. Good friends want me to remember that You're important. Amen.

BEST IDEA EVER

*"Do not steal. Be honest in what
you do. Do not lie to one another."*
LEVITICUS 19:11

You don't want me to take advantage of people, Lord Jesus. I can lie, steal, and cheat, but none are choices You want me to make. How can people learn to trust me if I keep telling them things that aren't true, taking what's theirs, and acting like these are the best ideas I've ever had? How will people trust You if they hear that I follow You and then I treat them badly? The laws You give me to follow aren't made to make life hard for me; they make life better for me and for others. I want people to see You when they see the choices I make. I don't want to make selfish choices that make me look bad and reflect poorly on You. I can't imagine You lying, stealing, or being dishonest with me. Help me do what You would do so that people see my good works and want to get to know You. Amen.

ONE MORE REALLY GOOD CHOICE

You have never been tempted to sin in any different way than other people. God is faithful. He will not allow you to be tempted more than you can take. But when you are tempted, He will make a way for you to keep from falling into sin.
1 Corinthians 10:13

I'm introduced to sin every day, Lord. I can find it on my own, people can point it out to me, and Your enemy Satan loves to make sin seem like a great choice. Everyone finds sin the same way. We all have the same struggles. We also all have the opportunity to get help. You can make me strong, but if the temptation to sin is too much, then You step in. You say that I don't have to make the wrong choice—even when I really want to. Help me remember that no matter how much I think I have no choice, You have made an escape plan that can help me move from disobedience to one more really good choice. Amen.

A NAME REMEMBERED

*A good name is to be chosen
instead of many riches. Favor is
better than silver and gold.*
PROVERBS 22:1

You want my choices to show that I care about what You think, Jesus. But You want me to care about what other people think too. You want me to care about whether people see the connection between You and me. You want my name to be remembered for the love I have for You. It's so wonderful to think that people can find You because You show up in my life. I wouldn't trade this for anything, and I'm willing to place all my trust, my choices, and my future in Your hands. Take care of things as I walk with You. I trust that You know the way and want me to find it. Help me remember how special Your name is so that when I tell others about You, they understand Jesus is a name I honor. Amen.

TRUTH CHASERS

Buy truth, and do not sell it. Get wisdom and teaching and understanding.
PROVERBS 23:23

I could spend the rest of my life working to earn enough money to buy truth, Lord. I could, but it would be useless, because You give truth for free. Some people would rather spend money trying to get truth. I can't sell Your truth, because I don't own it; but I can give it away. I want wisdom, so help me seek wisdom. I want You to teach me, Jesus, so help me learn. I want to understand, so help me use my mind. Your truth can change what I do, when I do it, and why I made the choice. Give me all the truth You can. Teach me again, because I'm sure I missed something. Keep teaching me every day until I meet You in heaven. I want to make knowing You the most important thing in my life. What I believe is important to You. What I learn means I am paying attention. What I share means I care for people You care about too. Amen.

I'M NOT THINKING WELL

For all men have sinned and have
missed the shining-greatness of God.
ROMANS 3:23

You promise Your "shining-greatness," Lord, but I settle for sin way too often. I miss the target of a good choice, even when I know what that good choice should be. Sometimes I just don't want to try, or I feel like I will miss out on something really good if I do what You say. I admit, I'm just not thinking very well. I forget some of Your promises. I forget that You have given instructions for how to live. I only remember that You forgive. I am forgetting way too many things. I need to spend more time with You to learn Your ways. I want to do what I should do. You don't ever leave me alone to make a bad choice—I do that all on my own. I have been wrong not to follow You. Help me make good choices today, Lord Jesus. Amen.

GETTING WHAT YOU DON'T DESERVE

Christ suffered and died for sins once for all. He never sinned and yet He died for us who have sinned. He died so He might bring us to God. His body died but His spirit was made alive.
1 PETER 3:18

Sin always gets the death penalty, Jesus. Sometimes I forget that. You can't let sin into heaven or it wouldn't be any different than here on earth. Because all humans sin, You had to do something about it. Humans were in a bad place, and our hopeless situation mattered to You. That's why You left heaven to come to earth to die on the cross. You took my death penalty. You are perfect, never sinned, and didn't deserve to die. But when You did, You invited people just like me to accept Your payment for sin. Your body died, but Your spirit couldn't. You rose from the dead so I could be forgiven and spend forever in heaven. That's a gift I don't deserve, so all I can say is, "Thank You!" Amen.

GROWING PAINS

*Then we will not be as children any longer.
Children are like boats thrown up and down on
big waves. They are blown with the wind. False
teaching is like the wind. False teachers try
everything possible to make people believe a lie,
but we are to hold to the truth with love in our
hearts. We are to grow up and be more like Christ.*
EPHESIANS 4:14–15

I don't have to believe everything people tell me, Lord. You don't even want me to. It's easy to think someone might be telling the truth. I might like what they say or it just sounds believable. But if You say it's not true, then it's not true. I'm going to keep growing up, and maybe it will become easier to tell the difference between truth and a made-up story. Help me grow up. I don't want to believe the wrong thing about what matters to You, Lord Jesus. I want to agree that what matters to You is most important—for me. Amen.

I LOVE A GOOD ADVENTURE

Teach me Your way, O Lord.
I will walk in Your truth.
PSALM 86:11

I want to make a promise to You, Lord. I know that by making this promise I may not keep it perfectly. But I want You to know that I think it's important to follow You, and I want to follow You well. Your truth is important, and I want to believe it. Your way is important, and I want to walk in Your way. I don't want to sit back and say, "That's too hard. I could never do that." But I am weak and You are strong, so please help me to keep the promise I want to make today. Forgive me when I fail, and keep pointing me in the right direction. My life is a quest, and I love a good adventure. You teach—I'll learn. You share truth—I'll believe it. You lead the way—I'll walk with You. Thanks for being a friend and for sharing Your life and love with me, Lord Jesus. Amen.

THIS MOUTH

Lips that tell the truth will last forever,
but a lying tongue lasts only for a little while.
PROVERBS 12:19

My mouth can be a beast, Jesus. It can say the cruelest things imaginable. It can be disrespectful to people I should respect. It can lie when the truth needs to be told. It can even twist kind words to hurt someone. But this mouth You gave me can be used for something better, and I want to use it the way You meant for it to be used. I will not always get it right, but I want to be willing to try. With Your teaching, I can change the way I speak, because You change the way I think—and that changes everything. When that happens, maybe it will be easier to speak words people will want to hear me say, words I will be proud to speak, and words that please You. Amen.

THE GREAT PRESCRIPTION

Jesus. . .said to them, "People who are well do not need a doctor. Only those who are sick need a doctor. I have not come to call those who are right with God. I have come to call those who are sinners."
MARK 2:17

I need You, Jesus. That must mean I'm not in perfect spiritual health. I want to be. I *need* to be. But I'm not—I never have been. You died on the cross for someone like me. You wouldn't need to help me if I didn't need help. The truth is, I break Your rules and I can't seem to stop. My spiritual health needs a checkup, and my spiritual life needs a new and very different plan. You're the only one who can provide the perfect checkup and plan for me. I'm no good at just trying my best to be better. I will need Your prescription to change the way I live. Thank You, Jesus. Amen.

SIN IS NOT OVERLOOKED

*[Jesus said,] "Go on your
way and do not sin again."*
JOHN 8:11

You don't celebrate sin, Lord Jesus. You don't overlook it or act as if it's not important. My obedience matters to You. You met a woman who sinned, and she expected You to be like everyone else and tell her that she was a horrible person. But You didn't. You told her that it was a good thing to go on with her life, but You finished by saying, "Do not sin again." No, You don't overlook sin, but You look at me. You love me. I matter to You. We are still friends, because You made a way to forgive me and then remind me, "Do not sin again." But if I do, You *still* offer forgiveness and You love me enough to remind me that sinning has never been what You want for me. Help me come back to You and refuse to hide. Help me stay close, because I need Your encouragement, Lord. Amen.

I STILL BROKE YOUR LAW

*If we tell Him our sins, He is faithful and we
can depend on Him to forgive us of our sins.
He will make our lives clean from all sin.*
1 JOHN 1:9

You are faithful, trustworthy, and dependable,
Lord. You know when I sin and get filthy, leav-
ing my soul needing more than the best wipe
can clean. I might try to pay for my sin by doing
more good than bad, but I have still done the
wrong thing. I can't make things even with You.
I can't make things right just by trying harder.
But I can be declared, "Not guilty!" because You
died on the cross to forgive me and clean my life
from every speck, spot, and stain of sin. The only
thing I have been able to do on my own is make
it worse—and so I will trust Your dependability
and find joy in Your forgiveness. Thank You, Jesus! Amen.

MAKE ME AN ANSWERED PRAYER

[Jesus said,] "For sure, I tell you,
anyone who gives a cup of cold water
to one of these little ones because he
follows Me, will not lose his reward."
MATTHEW 10:42

If You were to show up and spend the day walking and talking with me, Lord, I can only imagine what that day would be like. If I were hurt, You could heal me. If I were hungry, You could feed me. If I were thirsty, You could bring me a sparkling clean river. But I don't need to see You to know that You *do* walk and talk with me every day that I choose to walk with You and every day that I choose to read what You say in the Bible. Help me share the good things You do for me. And if someone is thirsty, I could get a bottle of water and make it my gift. Sometimes this is how You answer other people when they pray for a need. I would love the chance to be an answered prayer, Jesus. Amen.

SHE GAVE EVERYTHING

[Jesus] said, "I tell you the truth, this poor woman has put in more than all of them. For they have put in a little of the money they had no need for. She is very poor and has put in all she had. She has put in what she needed for her own living."
LUKE 21:3–4

I don't need to be better than anyone to do what You ask, Jesus. You don't hold contests to find out who could pray the longest, give the most, or do more good things than anyone else. What You really want to know is whether I will obey and if I love You enough to be generous with what You've given me. The widow You met was that kind of person. She was poor yet gave everything she had. She gave it *all* back to You. If everything I have is a gift from You, then I don't want to think twice about sharing any of it with You. Amen.

KEEPING WHAT
SHOULD BE SHARED

*Tell those who are rich in this world not to be
proud and not to trust in their money. Money
cannot be trusted. They should put their
trust in God. He gives us all we need for
our happiness. Tell them to do good and be
rich in good works. They should give much
to those in need and be ready to share.*
1 Timothy 6:17–18

When I brag about what I have, I'm trusting the wrong thing, Jesus. Money can't save me, and it won't love me. It lets me have things, but it takes away more than it gives, and what it gives never lasts. But You give me everything I need, and I'm satisfied. I want to help with things people need by using what You give me to use—not keep. What You have is worth so much more than anything I can carry in a wallet or use to fill a coin jar. Keep reminding me of this, because I will be tempted to keep what You want me to share. Amen.

SEE ME FOLLOW

Let no one show little respect for you because you are young. Show other Christians how to live by your life. They should be able to follow you in the way you talk and in what you do.
1 Timothy 4:12

I am not old, Lord. I have not lived a long time. I don't even have stories filled with years of following You on this amazing journey. Maybe I will someday. But today I love You; and I'm learning, so please keep teaching me. You say I can even show others what it looks like to follow You. I don't have to wait even one more day. No matter how old I am, I can tell others that they can follow You too. That's important. It might be easier to stay quiet, because I think I'm too young to tell people about You. But if people need to *see* someone following You before they're willing to *hear* about You, then let that person they see be me. I shouldn't be surprised if they join me in following You, Lord Jesus. Amen.

A TIME TO GROW UP

*When I was a child, I spoke like a child. I thought
like a child. I understood like a child. Now I
am a man. I do not act like a child anymore.*
1 CORINTHIANS 13:11

There are times when I want my way, Lord. I have
to admit that might have been recently. I can be
stubborn. I can throw fits sometimes too. I know
kids do that; but if I want people to notice You
when they see me, then I need Your help to grow
up. I don't want people to think that those who
claim to follow You are selfish. You don't want
that either. It's important to You that I'm kind
and show people what Your love looks like. Help
me to think like a grown-up Christian. Help me
to understand and obey You. You don't want me
to act like a baby Christian forever, Jesus, so I
really need Your help to grow up. Amen.

CHASE THE ADVENTURE

Anyone who lives on milk cannot understand the teaching about being right with God. He is a baby. Solid food is for full-grown men. They have learned to use their minds to tell the difference between good and bad.
HEBREWS 5:13–14

Milk tastes good, Jesus. It's easy to swallow. It's what most kids drink when they are little. Though it would be weird if milk were all I had for food now. There's lots of new food I like, and milk just doesn't keep me full like it used to. New Christians drink spiritual milk. It's how we start growing in You. We take in some things You teach, but some things are harder to understand. That might take time—and a new diet. There will be things I have to chew on or think about a little bit more. This is spiritual food that I need to learn to eat, but it's important to You that I learn. In my life with You, I want to grow up, be strong, and really experience this great adventure You have planned for me. Amen.

EVEN GREATER THINGS AHEAD

We are to hold to the truth with love in our hearts. We are to grow up and be more like Christ. He is the leader of the church.
EPHESIANS 4:15

Jesus, You never said, "I don't want to help those people." You did the hardest thing ever. You came to live right here on this planet. You experienced what it was like to be human. You did it because You loved people—You loved *me*. You were honorable, responsible, and humble. You're my example—the *very best* example. I want to grow up to be just like You, Jesus. Doing the easy things is a good place to start, but You've always wanted to see me trust You more so You could do even greater things in my life. Showing Your love to other people is just one way to prove that I'm growing up. Jesus, You are the leader, and I'm the follower. Help me pay attention to what You do so I can do the same. Amen.

OFF THE BENCH
AND IN THE GAME

"If anyone wants to serve Me, he must follow Me. So where I am, the one who wants to serve Me will be there also. If anyone serves Me, My Father will honor him."
JOHN 12:26

If I want to spend time with You, Lord, then I need to pay attention to what You do. It's important that I go where You go and see what You see. I can't just know that You're good and then not pay attention to what You're good at. If I play sports or sing, it's a good thing when someone I know shows up to see me do what I've been working so hard to learn. The same is true for You. Although You don't need an audience, learning from You helps me do more than sit in the stands and applaud. I want to serve You. Help me follow You and watch what You do. And then help me serve to the best of my ability with You in the lead. Amen.

HIS BEST IS
PERFECTLY AMAZING

*[Jesus said,] "You are bad and you know
how to give good things to your children.
How much more will your Father in heaven
give good things to those who ask Him?"*

MATTHEW 7:11

I don't always do the right thing, Jesus. But sometimes I can be pretty nice all on my own. It never lasts; but even when I don't choose to follow You, I can do the right thing from time to time. Maybe that's because You made all people to want to be close to You, and doing good is one way we try. If my best is pretty good, then Your best is perfectly *amazing*. When there's something I really need and then I ask You for help, You don't hold back if the answer is yes. Sometimes You give even more than I ever thought possible. You aren't just good *some* of the time. You are *always* good, *always* kind, *always* helpful. Always. And that will always matter to me. Amen.

COURSE CHANGE

A wise son listens when his father tells him the right way, but one who laughs at the truth does not listen when strong words are spoken to him.
PROVERBS 13:1

To grow up, I need to pay attention, Jesus. Things are happening all around me, and it all matters. Help me learn what I need to learn. People can teach me some of what I need to know, but most of what I need to learn comes from You. If I'm wise, I'll listen with my ears wide open. I'll keep my mouth closed, even when I think what I hear isn't needed or is just too unbelievable. I understand that sometimes You'll have to correct my thinking. Help me take Your lesson and make it a blessing. You aren't punishing me when You tell me to change direction. You're changing the course of my life, and it's always better when I follow Your way, Lord. Live in me. Help my life speak Your truth. And help me recognize when Your class is in session. Amen.

I ALWAYS HAVE YOU

*"Love those who hate you. (*Respect and give thanks for those who say bad things to you. Do good to those who hate you.) Pray for those who do bad things to you and who make it hard for you."*
MATTHEW 5:44

No one likes it when mean people show up, Lord. But You never tell me to leave them out just because they are mean. You actually tell me to love these people—even if they hate me. They don't realize that when they act mean they're just pointing me to You. When I'm struggling, You mean more to me than ever before. You're amazing, and Your kindness is so much better than the reminders of meanness. I think even mean people want to know there's good somewhere in their world. And just maybe You want that to come from me. Give me the courage to give kindness even when I seem to receive something less friendly in return; because, no matter what, I'll always have You, Jesus. Amen.

THE KIND LIFE

[Jesus said,] "If the world hates you,
you know it hated Me before it hated you."
JOHN 15:18

Just when I think I'm the only one who has to deal with mean people, Jesus, I read that You have too. People hated You long before they were ever mean to me. That doesn't mean we should start a club for people who get picked on. You want me to be strong and realize that You have a message that some people don't like. Some people are frightened that You might be real. Some people have been hurt by someone else, and they think being mean is normal. They can't change if everyone returns meanness for meanness. That kind of life just makes people tired. They have no joy, and they're never satisfied. I don't want to be that way; but because some people are that way, it encourages me to pray for the ones who hate me, the ones who hate You, and everyone who could just use a whole lot more of You, Lord. Amen.

THE GREAT, FULL LIFE

*"I am the Door. Anyone who goes in through
Me will be saved from the punishment of sin.
He will go in and out and find food. The robber
comes only to steal and to kill and to destroy.
I came so they might have life, a great full life."*
JOHN 10:9–10

A great, full life? That's what I want, Lord Jesus. You can make it possible, but You don't pass out a "great, full life" to just anyone You want to; people have to want it too. You are the door that swings wide open to welcome people; but some shut the door, walk around You, or mutter something about why people leave doors open. They totally miss You. How does that happen? It seems so easy—and it is—but it's even easier to think about the struggles we face when we don't see You and don't understand what You can do. My search ended when I asked You into my heart—and my great, full life has led to a most excellent and grateful life. Amen.

FAIRY TALES ABOUT REAL PEOPLE

See that no one misses God's loving-favor.
Do not let wrong thoughts about others
get started among you. If you do, many
people will be turned to a life of sin.
HEBREWS 12:15

I hear stories, Lord, and sometimes I believe them. They are told about people I know, and my mind thinks what I heard could *possibly* be true. I don't ask if it really is true, but I choose to believe what I'm told—and then I share it with others. That's called "gossip." And when I tell tall tales, the person who hears my story misses out on Your loving favor because they don't see any love in my storytelling. Some people become mean people because wrong thoughts lead to wrong words and wrong conclusions. So I should treat people kindly, share Your truth openly, and love others deeply. Help me avoid telling fairy tales about real people, Jesus. Amen.

A CHOSEN LIFE

*You are a chosen group of people. You are the
King's religious leaders. You are a holy nation.
You belong to God. He has done this for you
so you can tell others how God has called
you out of darkness into His great light.*
1 PETER 2:9

You chose me, and I belong to You, Jesus. You call Yourself "light," and You encouraged me to leave darkness behind. I'm glad You did, because I had no idea where I was going, I kept stumbling, and I was unable to help anyone else. I'm on Your team, and I want to work with my family to get the word out that "Jesus is good, and everyone should get to know Him!" Use me to help show people that You offer light at the end of their tunnel. Give me courage to walk with You, talk with You, and tell everyone I meet that You matter to me. I love You, Lord. Help me keep looking for Your light when it seems like most people keep stumbling in the dark. Amen.

A WALKING PARTNER

"They were to look for God. Then they might feel after Him and find Him because He is not far from each one of us."
ACTS 17:27

When I have to get up in the middle of the night, Lord Jesus, I can't see. I use my hand to feel for the light switch. When I find it and flip the switch, I can suddenly see all the things that would have caused me to stumble if I had left the lights off. I know where to go when the light is on, and I don't have to second-guess where to put my feet. Light is important to You because it's a picture of You. Darkness is not. You don't hide in the shadows, trying to scare people. That's not You. You want people like me to look for You and find You, so we can leave the spiritual shadows and dark nights behind. You don't walk six steps ahead, Lord. Your pace is easy, and having You as a walking partner is amazingly helpful. Let's keep walking together! Amen.

THE ANSWER TO QUESTIONS

The Lord has looked down from heaven
on the sons of men, to see if there are
any who understand and look for God.
PSALM 14:2

You keep an eye out for boys like me—boys who are looking for You, Lord. Am I learning? Am I seeking? Am I making You my best friend? I could come a little closer. And if I did, how would that help me? How would it please You? I have questions that only You can answer. When I make choices because I've found good answers, then I can stay closer to You—the one who looked for me to see if I was looking for Him. I know You want to be found. I know You don't hide. I'm beginning to understand that my choice to follow pleases You and helps me. So, yes, I'm learning. Yes, I'm seeking. And I do want You for my best friend. Thanks for watching me grow. Amen.

EVERYTHING I
NEED TO BELIEVE

A man cannot please God unless he has faith. Anyone who comes to God must believe that He is. That one must also know that God gives what is promised to the one who keeps on looking for Him.
HEBREWS 11:6

I don't want to make the choice to believe that You don't exist, Jesus. Faith is important to You, and You give me everything I need to believe that You exist, that You are a promise keeper, and that I can find You. Faith says I believe that You can rescue someone like me from the bad choices I make. Faith says I believe You can forgive me when I break Your rules. Faith says that someday I will see You with my own eyes, and I will never have to go back to the way things were. Faith asks me to keep walking and never give up. Faith prepares me for another day when I look forward to spending time with You. Thank You, Lord. Amen.

WHAT IF

"Everyone who asks receives what he asks for. Everyone who looks finds what he is looking for. Everyone who knocks has the door opened to him."
MATTHEW 7:8

What if the first thing I ask for is rescue, Jesus? What if the first thing I find is You? What if the door I knock on is Yours? What if? . . . You want to rescue, be discovered, and You welcome the interested. I don't want to try to imagine what life would be like without You—and I don't have to, because I do know You, Lord. There are other people who want to know You, but they aren't sure if it's even possible. Maybe they're afraid to seek answers to those "What if" questions. You just want to know if they're interested enough to ask, look, and knock. When they do, You make sure they receive, find, and are welcome. I needed that, and now I don't have to ask the "What if" questions. Being found is important to You. Finding You is important to me. Amen.

THE GOOD CHOICE

I will praise You with a heart that is
right when I learn how right You judge.

PSALM 119:7

I need to be honest with You, Lord. I don't always understand everything You do and why You do it the way You do. But it's important that You make the choices You need to make. I'm grateful that You don't make choices the way I would make them, because I've made some really bad choices. You know so much more than I do—more than I will ever know. The proof of Your good choices comes up much later when the good things get separated from the bad. The way You take care of issues is much different from the way I would do things. Help me remember that when You make a choice, it's *always* going to be a good choice. Your choices always start with the love You have for people like me, and they never stop. Thank You. Amen.

BE THE EXAMPLE

"Go and make followers of all the nations."
Matthew 28:19

To be a follower, I'll need an example, Jesus. That's You. To invite people to become Your followers, I'll need to be an example. I can't ask people to join this adventure with You if they can't see any difference in me. Why would anyone make a choice that's supposed to help them if they can't tell that I've been helped? They wouldn't! It's important to You that I follow first and then keep following, so other people know what that looks like. If I'm supposed to go to people and ask them to follow You, then they'll need to see me follow first. I won't be able to help anyone learn more about You if I don't know You very well. Maybe that's why You ask me to follow before You ask me to do anything else. You did that with Your disciples, and You still do that with Your followers today. Amen.

LISTEN AND ENCOURAGE

Comfort each other and
make each other strong.
1 Thessalonians 5:11

It's important that Christians get along, Lord Jesus. If people don't mean much to me, then I won't listen to them; I won't help when they need help; and I won't be friendly when they need a friend. Instead, I'll just do what I want and not pay attention to anyone—not even You. That's not Your solution, because what I want probably won't even really help me. The words I use can either help people feel better or make them feel worse. These words can take what little strength they have away, or they might make them bold enough to look for and ask about You. Use me to speak truth, offer kindness, and encourage friends. Make me the kind of boy people want to talk to. Maybe they'll feel better because I was willing to listen and because I was willing to encourage them. Amen.

STRENGTH FOR
A LITTLE LONGER

*Good news from a land far away
is like cold water to a tired soul.*
PROVERBS 25:25

Playing outside on a hot day is fun, Jesus. I don't need a jacket, and I never get cold. But I do get thirsty. When I'm offered a juice box or a bottle of water, I down it in a hurry and am thankful someone took care of my thirst. Then I get back out there and play a little longer. Sometimes, if someone doesn't offer a drink, I will keep playing until I feel sick from not drinking enough water. My body needed water and didn't get it. That's never good. You say that Your good news is important because it does for my soul what water does for my body. When encouragement is hard to find and my soul needs a drink, You send me encouragement. It satisfies, refreshes, and makes me strong enough to get back out there and tell others about You for a little longer. Amen.

WHO WOULDN'T?

We have been pure. We have known what to do. We have suffered long. We have been kind. The Holy Spirit has worked in us. We have had true love.
2 CORINTHIANS 6:6

How people remember me matters, Lord. If I make what I learn personal, I want people to say, "He was pure. He made good choices. When he suffered, He trusted God. He was kind. God's Spirit worked in Him. He always showed true love." Who wouldn't want to be that kind of guy? Who wouldn't want to be remembered that way? Who wouldn't live this kind of life and be satisfied? People might remember this kind of guy for a long time and for good reasons. I want to do something more than impress people. I want them to see You in the choices I make so they will want to choose You. I want that to be more important than how people might remember me. I think that's exactly what You want for me too. Amen.

SPEAK GOOD WORDS

*Watch your talk! No bad words should be
coming from your mouth. Say what is good.
Your words should help others grow as Christians.*
EPHESIANS 4:29

Careless words never help anyone, Jesus. I admit
I've spoken many careless words. Sometimes it's
been sarcasm, mean jokes, or rude comments. I
say words that I know might hurt someone, but I
also think other people will believe my words are
funny. I need Your help to convince my mind and
heart to send good words to my mouth. Help
my mouth speak good words. Help those who
hear these words understand and value them so
much that they are sad when they hear anything
else come from my heart, mind, and mouth. You
spoke some wonderful words, and I can read
them anytime I read the Bible. I want Your words
to make a difference in how I speak, and I want
what I speak to make a difference in how other
people hear. And I want what people hear from
me to make a difference in what they believe.
Amen.

THE GIVING KEEPS ON

If someone has the gift of speaking words of comfort and help, he should speak. If someone has the gift of sharing what he has, he should give from a willing heart. If someone has the gift of leading other people, he should lead them. If someone has the gift of showing kindness to others, he should be happy as he does it.
ROMANS 12:8

Gifts are meant to be shared, Lord. You shared some with me. Give me the courage to share some with others—gifts like giving encouragement, doing what I can to help when help is needed, being a leader, and showing kindness. You give me these kinds of gifts because I need them and because I can share them without losing any of what I already have. I can be kind today, and I can still be kind tomorrow. I can encourage today and do the same tomorrow. I can . . .because You're kind and encouraging today and will be tomorrow too! Amen.

WHY DO I EVEN TRY?

We ask you, Christian brothers, speak to those who do not want to work. Comfort those who feel they cannot keep going on. Help the weak. Understand and be willing to wait for all men.

1 Thessalonians 5:14

Sometimes I don't want to go to school, Jesus. I don't want to talk to people. I don't want to obey. I just want to be left alone. I could be angry, sad, or just really frustrated. Someone could have been mean to me, or I might have gotten a bad grade on a test. I want to give up and ask, "Why do I even try?" What I really need is for You to send someone to talk me through this hard place and time. And when I come through hard days because You sent the help I needed, then help me to be the one who encourages, comforts, and walks with people who ask the question I recognize: "Why do I even try?" You have the answers I need, Lord, and I am thankful. Amen.

IN THE BEGINNING

The Word (Christ) was in the beginning.
The Word was with God. The Word was God.
John 1:1

You have always existed. It can be easy to think You showed up for the first time when You were born. But when this world was created for people, You were already here—and just as powerful and important as You are now. You knew that people would need to be rescued from the bad choices they would make—and we make them *a lot*. You matter to every part of the human story. You know what it's like to be human. You're the only one who has ever really seen life as God *and* as a person. You understood what it was like to be hungry and thirsty. You were tempted to make bad choices. Humans die, and You did too; but because You are just like God, You couldn't stay dead. Because You know what it's like to be a person, You help the same way God helps. You and God are one and the same. Amen.

THE BATTLE

The things our old selves want to do are against what the Holy Spirit wants. The Holy Spirit does not agree with what our sinful old selves want. These two are against each other.
GALATIANS 5:17

There is a fight going on inside me, Lord. I get to pick sides. I can choose the enemy who fights against everything You want, or I can choose You. It may seem like a no-brainer—I should choose You, but sometimes I don't. Sometimes I almost find myself cheering for Your enemy, and I can't come up with a good reason for cheering. When I don't cheer for You, I find myself making the bad choice Your enemy says I should make. But You fight this battle for me. Your enemy wants me to fall down and stay down. He wants You to lose; and if You didn't fight for me, I would have no hope because I cannot fight Your enemy on my own. When I try, I always fail. Standing with You is not only a good idea, Jesus, it's an honor. Amen.

I WANT TO DO GOOD

I do not do the good I want to do.
Instead, I am always doing the
sinful things I do not want to do.
ROMANS 7:19

Without Your help, I'll make plenty of bad choices, Jesus. Sin is the name of every bad choice I make, because sin is all the things that break Your rules. That's what makes sin a very bad choice. Bad choices are the things I do that You don't want me to do—and then I'm not even sure why I do them. I make bad choices even when I want to make good ones. It's the battle going on inside me, and sometimes I can pay too much attention to the wrong side. I want to do good; but when I don't, it's usually because I either don't know what You want or I don't want to do what You want. Could You help me pay more attention to You so the good choices You want me to make are easier for me to make? Thank You! Amen.

DON'T FORGET

Do you forget about His loving-kindness to you?
Do you forget how long He is waiting for you?
You know that God is kind. He is trying to get you
to be sorry for your sins and turn from them.
ROMANS 2:4

You don't want me to forget, Jesus. Please keep my mind thinking about You. It matters. It's important. I can get busy and forget that You're kind. I can have a long to-do list and forget that You're waiting for me to show up so we can talk like we're doing right now. You don't just want me to *say* I'm sorry. You want me to *be* sorry. When I say the words but don't really mean them, I will never change. When I mean them, I'll actually do something more than say words I think You want to hear. When I'm sad because I chose not to follow Your instructions, I'll probably learn to pay more attention to what You say. That's what I want to do, Lord. Amen.

MOVING DAY

Put out of your life all these things: bad feelings about other people, anger, temper, loud talk, bad talk which hurts other people, and bad feelings which hurt other people. You must be kind to each other. Think of the other person. Forgive other people just as God forgave you because of Christ's death on the cross.
EPHESIANS 4:31–32

I have things in my life that need to go, Lord. Make it moving day. I don't have space for my bad feelings collection. Anger stands in the way of kindness, so it needs to leave. My temper doesn't make enough room for love. Loud talk makes it hard to hear Your whisper. My collection of words has hurt too many people. Many things are taking up too much space. I need more room for You. Help me to choose kindness, love, and forgiveness, because they always leave room for You. But the other things? I don't need them, and You won't keep them. Help me be willing to leave them behind as I walk with You. Amen.

JUST LIKE YOU

*No person who has become a child of
God keeps on sinning. This is because the
Holy Spirit is in him. He cannot keep on
sinning because God is his Father.*

1 JOHN 3:9

The longer I walk with You, the fewer bad choices
I want to make, Jesus. I should sin less the
longer we walk together. That's because You
continue to teach me, and what I learn helps
me understand the things that disappoint You.
I want to stay away from the bad choices that
leave You sad. I need to grow up and make time
to learn from You. I don't need to wait. Let the
teaching begin. I want to grow up to be just
like You. I have Your example. I have Your truth
in my Bible. It's important for me to know what
my family stands for. Thank You, Lord Jesus. Amen.

WORK TO TEACH ME

*Those who let their sinful old selves tell them
what to do live under that power of their sinful
old selves. But those who let the Holy Spirit
tell them what to do are under His power.*
ROMANS 8:5

There will always be someone to give me directions, Jesus. I want it to be You; but I have taken directions from someone who refuses to follow You—Your enemy, the devil. He can't make me sin, but he is quick to tell me why he thinks breaking Your rules is a good idea. The first man and woman on earth listened to him, and then every person who has ever been born has heard from him too. Even You heard from the devil. The enemy tried to make You believe it made sense to break God's rules. But You paid attention to God and what He knew was true. He never believed the enemy's arguments. I don't have to believe them either. Help me choose to do what the Holy Spirit works to teach me. Amen.

BENEFITS

If your sinful old self is the boss over your mind, it leads to death. But if the Holy Spirit is the boss over your mind, it leads to life and peace.
ROMANS 8:6

I will always work for a boss, Jesus. Even if I one day own and run a business, I will still have a boss. I will hear from that boss every day. I even get to choose who will be my boss. My boss could be the things I learned when sin was my first choice, or it could be You. If I listen to my sinful past, it will ask me to go back to familiar sin. If I listen to You, I will be asked to think new thoughts about old struggles. When I let the Holy Spirit set rules for me to follow, You promise good things like life and peace. I like both of those benefits. But when I let my sinful past boss me around, it only ends in the death of things like friendships and Your good plans for me. Amen.

PEOPLE WHO DON'T UNDERSTAND

How long must I plan what to do in my soul, and have sorrow in my heart all the day? How long will those who hate me rise above me?
PSALM 13:2

When You are my boss, there will be people who don't understand, Lord Jesus. They might say that only children follow You, and that works for me because I started following You as a child. I can be sad when I know that not everyone will be happy with my good choice. I might even see that some people have an easy life while they keep away from You. Some people who used to like me might hate me now, because I follow You. I can be disappointed if I think that my life needs to look like their lives. But the good things You give me may not look like what other people have. You promised to meet my needs, and then You promised always to keep me company. That's something I'll always have. It's something others are missing out on. Thank You, Lord. Amen.

YOU NEVER TALK BAD ABOUT ME

"The one who loves Me is the one who has My teaching and obeys it. My Father will love whoever loves Me. I will love him and will show Myself to him."
JOHN 14:21

I can show that I love You, and it will mean more than words, Lord. Saying that I love You sounds good, but some people don't think words are proof of anything. These people will do some investigation to see if what I say is true. If they hear me say I love You and then see me doing things they know You said is off limits, they'll have trouble believing anything I say about You. This matters to You, because You love me so much and You're never embarrassed to be with me. You never talk bad about me. Help me show that I love You by knowing what You say and then doing what You ask. I don't want to be embarrassed by You. I want to follow Your instructions without complaining. Amen.

A SHOW OF RESPECT

Obey the head leader of the country and all other leaders over you. This pleases the Lord. Obey the men who work for them. God sends them to punish those who do wrong and to show respect to those who do right.
1 PETER 2:13–14

You have asked me to do something very hard, Lord. You ask me to respect the leader of my country—and it doesn't matter who that leader is. Maybe if I don't respect the leader of my country, it would be easier for me to show disrespect to You. Maybe showing honor is a great example for others. Maybe You want to know if I will still obey You even when it's hard. I need to remember that even this is one of Your instructions. If I love You, I will obey by showing respect to the men and women who make hard choices for my country. Help me make the choice to pray for them. Please help them make good decisions. Amen.

MADE TO HELP

Help each other in troubles and problems.
This is the kind of law Christ asks us to obey.
GALATIANS 6:2

You never once said You only help those who help themselves, Jesus. You did say that You'll sometimes help people by sending someone like me to do what's needed. It's one of Your rules, and helping is very unselfish. It would be a very different world if You made rules that encouraged people to think only of themselves. Those rules would be much easier to follow, but then who would have any friends? Nobody would want to help anyone, and no one would trust anyone else. That's not how You want Your children to act. You want me to think about other people so much that when they struggle, I notice and try to help. You want me to depend on You, and You want other people to be able to depend on me. Being dependable matters to You—and it matters to everyone I'll ever meet. Amen.

THE SMART CHOICE

"Whoever hears these words of Mine and does not do them, will be like a foolish man."
MATTHEW 7:26

You tell me the truth, Lord Jesus. The last thing You want me to do when I hear Your rules is to say, "Now that's interesting, but I just don't feel like it." That would be a really foolish thing to do, but still I sometimes do it. It doesn't seem like I trust You when You tell me there's something better if I'll just do what You say but I say, "Nope." I know I'm not as wise as You, so any reason I have for not obeying is not a smart choice. If someone important asked me to do something for them, I would be happy to say yes. So I don't know why it makes sense to say no to You. I want to be wise and not foolish, Lord. Amen.

SHOW THAT MY HEART HAS CHANGED

"Do something to show me that your hearts are changed."
MATTHEW 3:8

When I hear what You want, it's important that I do something about it, Lord. But what do I do? How do I do it? You give good information that I'm happy to think about for a very long time, as long as I don't have to do anything about it right now. I think most people are that way. But it doesn't change what I choose to do, does it? What can I do today that shows that You've changed my heart, mind, and choices? You've already told me. I know the answer, but I've been ignoring You. I've made the wrong choice. I need to do what You ask so I can be what You want me to be. Help me do something I know I need to do, so I can show You that my heart is changing and then tell others so they can do the same thing. Amen.

NO NEED FOR A NAP

Get your minds ready for good use. Keep awake.
Set your hope now and forever on the loving-favor
to be given you when Jesus Christ comes again.
1 PETER 1:13

My mind can make bad choices when my spirit takes a nap, Jesus. My spirit goes to sleep when I stop thinking about You. When I don't make You most important, my mind wanders, my heart stops caring, and my spirit sleeps. There's a lot going on, and I'm missing it. It seems like I don't really care that You're doing some amazing things. And even if I say that what You're doing is important, my choices don't show that I really believe it. So wake me up, Lord, and give me the wisdom to see the good things You do. Give my spirit the opportunity to praise You. And in the end, help me realize I need You every moment of every day. Amen.

A FULL HEART

"Good comes from a good man because of the riches he has in his heart. Sin comes from a sinful man because of the sin he has in his heart. The mouth speaks of what the heart is full of."
LUKE 6:45

My heart is full, Jesus. I'll share what's in there, but it may not be the greatest news. I can always share what's in my heart, but there are times I might be ashamed to talk about what You find there. Often what's in my heart is not You. Maybe that's why You say that the heart can lie to me. I struggle with staying close to You when I let things overtake my heart and move my thinking away from You. When You aren't in my heart, sin has a great opportunity to replace all the good You bring. Sin makes the bad look good, and it leaves marks I don't want. So, yes, Lord Jesus, my heart is always full. Help me let it be full—of You! Amen.

BACK TOMORROW

If you do not have wisdom, ask God for it.
He is always ready to give it to you and
will never say you are wrong for asking.
JAMES 1:5

When I need wisdom, You don't turn me down, Lord. That's good news, because I'll always need Your wisdom. My best idea will still fail when it's not what You want. And no matter how much I learn, it will never be a replacement for Your wisdom. You won't even say, "Didn't I give you wisdom last week? You've probably had enough." You don't keep for Yourself what You know I need. You aren't selfish. I don't have enough wisdom. Would You give me the wisdom I need today? I'll be back tomorrow. I'll keep looking for Your truth. I'll keep waiting for Your answers. I'll keep wanting what You want for me. You love me, and Your plan means more than mine, Jesus. Make Your wisdom one of my greatest requests. Make my heart Your home. Amen.

BE DIFFERENT

*Do not act like the sinful people of the world.
Let God change your life. First of all, let Him
give you a new mind. Then you will know what
God wants you to do. And the things you do
will be good and pleasing and perfect.*
ROMANS 12:2

Why would anyone want to change their life if
You don't offer anything different than what
they already experience, Lord? You're different,
and You want me to be the same kind of different. I shouldn't continue acting like I've always
acted, do what I've always done, or even make
choices the same way I've always made choices.
Change my mind, and it will change what I do,
where I go, and what I say. Help me see that this
new life will lead to choices that can be good,
pleasing, and perfect. This matters, because I
don't need to live life being something that I'm
not supposed to be. I want to be who I was created to be, Lord! Amen.

TRANSLATION REQUIRED

The person who is not a Christian does not understand these words from the Holy Spirit. He thinks they are foolish. He cannot understand them because he does not have the Holy Spirit to help him understand.

1 Corinthians 2:14

There was a time when I couldn't understand what You were saying, Lord. I saw people work for what they wanted, and You said that what You had for them was free and they couldn't buy it. I saw people take, and You said they should give to have what they need. I saw people get hurt, and You said they should forgive when most people thought it was a good idea to get even. Not much of what You said seemed to make sense, but then I understood why: You said your ways couldn't be understood by those who didn't let the Holy Spirit teach them. So before I became a Christian, Your teaching didn't make sense to me. Now it does, and I'm still learning. Please keep teaching me. Amen.

FOCUS ON HIS LIST

Christian brothers, keep your minds thinking about whatever is true, whatever is respected, whatever is right, whatever is pure, whatever can be loved, and whatever is well thought of. If there is anything good and worth giving thanks for, think about these things.

PHILIPPIANS 4:8

I'm learning to think differently, Lord. I'm learning to think about things that won't get me off track. You have given me a list, and each item matters to You. I need to think about truth, because lies cause damage. I need to show respect for people and things that are worthy of respect. Focusing on right and good things is wiser than chasing bad choices. Pure things are helpful, while things mixed with bad ingredients leave a bad taste. The things You ask me to love are greater than anyone I could choose to hate. When I focus on Your list, I can be grateful and my mind won't wander away from You. Amen.

GREAT IS BETTER THAN GOOD

I pray that you will know what is the very best. I pray that you will be true and without blame until the day Christ comes again.
PHILIPPIANS 1:10

You give me so many good things to enjoy, Jesus. Thank You. Sometimes I choose a *good* thing and miss out on something *great*. That's one more chance for the Holy Spirit to teach me. I can spend a lot of time doing something that doesn't break Your rules, but it doesn't get me any closer to You. I'm not led to the wrong place; I'm just sort of left in the same place. Help me learn that I don't have to settle for good things when You have *great* things I could be doing. I don't waste my time when I do good things; but when I learn to choose great things, the adventure grows and I become more responsible. Help me to always seek Your great choices even when I might be doing something good. Amen.

DON'T CRUMBLE, FOLD, OR BREAK

If a man lives a clean life, he will be like a dish made of gold. He will be respected and set apart for good use.
2 TIMOTHY 2:21

Food tastes good, Jesus. It gives me what I need to keep growing. You say that I'm like a plate—I could be a sturdy dinner plate that will hold the food and won't spill; or I could be a cheap paper plate that has trouble holding the food. You want me to be like a plate made of gold. It won't crumble, fold, or break. It will hold the food with no problems. People will want to use that plate. But I'm not really a plate, and I don't hold people's supper. But I do hold Your truth, and You want me to be sturdy and reliable in taking that truth to others so they can taste it and see that it's good. You want me to be used to share Your good news. With Your help, I won't crumble, fold, or break. Amen.

IN MY ROOM, DISTRACTED

*[Jesus] gave Himself as a perfect gift to
God through the Spirit that lives forever.
Now your heart can be free from the guilty
feeling of doing work that is worth nothing.
Now you can work for the living God.*
HEBREWS 9:14

I've been told to clean my room, Lord Jesus.
Sometimes I sit and do something different. I
might start cleaning but then get distracted by
something I find. I might play with it or think
about how silly it was to want it when I asked for
it. I may need to fold my clothes but find a ball
to play with, and my socks don't get folded. You
give me things to do too, and You don't want me
to leave them undone. I work for You, and what
I do matters. Help me accept the job You want
me to do and then ask for directions. Open my
heart to say yes, my mind to ask for help, and
my spirit to understand the good things that
come with obedience. Amen.

DON'T WAIT TO SHOW LOVE

*Love each other with a kind heart
and with a mind that has no pride.*
1 Peter 3:8

Loving other people makes me wonder what they ever did for me first, Jesus. That's the wrong way of thinking. The only one who ever needed to prove love first was You. Otherwise, no one would know how to love. Once I know that I'm loved by You, I can love others even if they don't like me. I don't have to wait for them to ask if we can be friends. I can show kindness without ever trying to impress them. You ask me to love. You ask other Christians to love me. And this kind of love helps others when it would be easier to say, "You made a mess of things. All the best getting out of that." I'm really glad You never do that to me. You made sure I understood that I matter to You. Then You made sure I knew that everyone else matters to You too. Amen.

FORGIVEN AND LOVED

Love each other as Christian brothers.
Show respect for each other.
ROMANS 12:10

I'm a child of God. All who follow You are His children. That makes them my Christian family. They're my brothers and sisters in faith. You don't want me to ignore them. Instead, I should honor them and show them respect. After all, they're following You. A good reason to be respectful is because if they follow You, then they're wise enough to know that they can't make good choices without You. I can't either. So my Christian family includes a group of broken people who know that You fix broken people. Even Christians make bad choices, but they know that You'll be the one who can help when they don't know what else to do. I can't expect other Christians to be perfect—just forgiven and loved by You. Amen.

I NEED TO LISTEN

*Nothing should be done because of pride
or thinking about yourself. Think of other
people as more important than yourself.*
PHILIPPIANS 2:3

When I meet someone, it's normal for me to want to tell them all about myself, Lord, but what if they don't need to hear my story? What if I need to hear their story instead? What if You want me to pay attention to their struggles? What if I gave them the gift of love that is kind and offers to listen? How would that change me? If I put the needs of other people before my own, then You can use me to help others and You'll listen to my struggles. If I do this, then You help two people at the same time. You need to know everything about me, but I don't need to demand that other people listen to my story. They might listen, and I'll be encouraged; but if they need to talk, then I need to listen. Thanks for showing me how to do that, Jesus. Amen.

LOVING THE IMPERFECT

Most of all, have a true love for each other.
1 PETER 4:8

I'm face-to-face with the one thing that's most important to You, Jesus: love. I don't just get to think about it today and forget it tomorrow. Love is Your greatest rule, and it's a choice You want me to make every single day. I choose to love You, and I choose to love people. You want my love to be real and true. You want me to offer love to everyone I meet. I don't get to choose who I think is lovable and worth the time and effort. I get to love the lonely, the sad, the misfit, the outcast, and the imperfect. That's everyone—and they are exactly who You want me to love. You don't leave people out, and You don't want me to do that either. Make me brave enough to love. I won't do this as well as You, but I do believe that love matters, Lord. Amen.

RUN THE RACE

*You know that only one person gets a crown
for being in a race even if many people run.
You must run so you will win the crown.*
1 Corinthians 9:24

Most people run a race to beat the competition, Jesus. You ask me to run a race, but the only competition I have is myself. The real goal of this race is finishing. If I leave the race to watch others run, then I'm not working to finish the race. If I join a different race, then I'm not running the only one worth winning. When I finish, I win. When other runners finish, they win. The prize is more than a participation ribbon. The winners remember the finish line, and they understand the race was worth it. The life You offer is worth it. The race matters, and I get to run with Your help—on Your path, in Your direction. Give me the courage to run and keep on running. Give me the strength to finish. Amen.

THE WINNER'S CROWN

*Everyone who runs in a race does many things
so his body will be strong. He does it to get
a crown that will soon be worth nothing, but
we work for a crown that will last forever.*
1 CORINTHIANS 9:25

When I watch sports, Lord Jesus, I see stories of athletes who get up early, stay up late, and spend most of their time working out so they can compete at the highest level possible. They give up free time to spend lifting weights, running ovals, and swimming laps. If they want to be the best, they have to do what most won't. They set records and win trophies only to see someone else break their records and replace their trophies, and these athletes that gave so much time and effort are often forgotten. The race You ask me to run is about spending time with You. When I finish, the winner's crown is mine, and no one can take it. It will always be a reminder of Your love for me. Amen.

THE COACH

*In the same way, I run straight for the place
at the end of the race. I fight to win.*
1 Corinthians 9:26

Some say I should look for light at the end of the tunnel, Jesus. It's their way of saying that the hard things I face will end at the finish line. The race won't last forever. The end of this race is the beginning of forever. It's when I meet You and see all that You've prepared for me at the end of the race. I keep running, because it matters to You. You set my feet on this racetrack and whispered in my ear that it was time to run. So I'm running. I want to win. One day my foot will step over the finish line, and You'll greet me and show me around Your home. This is a day that I'll enjoy because it'll be clear that You never left me, You never abandoned me, and You were my coach every step of my journey home. Amen.

WHAT I CAN

*I keep working over my body. I make it
obey me. I do this because I am afraid
that after I have preached the Good News
to others, I myself might be put aside.*
1 CORINTHIANS 9:27

I want to do what I can to finish this race, Jesus. I know You'll help me, and I don't doubt it for a minute. But I don't want to be lazy and think that the race doesn't matter. I don't want to hear that my actions meant that I was disqualified. What I want is to be committed to the race, determined to finish, and willing to obey. It's still Your racecourse, and I'm still able to get the help I need; but I want to cooperate with You by keeping my feet moving and by paying attention to where I'm going. I need to obey Your instructions. You do what only You can do, and I'll do everything I can to do what You ask. Amen.

EYES ON THE PRIZE

*My eyes are on the crown. I want to win
the race and get the crown of God's call
from heaven through Christ Jesus.*
PHILIPPIANS 3:14

I've prayed for help, Lord Jesus. I need to remember that there's a purpose for running this
race. It has a beginning where I'm eager to run
the race because it's new and exciting. There's
a middle to the race where I'm tired and un-
sure if I can keep running. It has an end where
I'll be invited to rest. I'll be declared the victor
and be satisfied that I didn't stop. I'll be grateful for Your friendship along the way. This race
takes encouragement, and You give it. This race
takes strength, and You supply it. This race takes
patience, and I'm learning it. The things that I'll
discover in this race cannot be learned as a spec-
tator. Make me willing to run. Make me excited
to learn. Help me to make the finish line a journey, destination, and life goal. Amen.

SAFE

*I am kept safe by God, Who saves
those who are pure in heart.*
PSALM 7:10

You never say that half of all people just need to do the best they can, Lord. You have a plan for *every single person.* There are never too many humans for You to love, and You don't have to make anyone wait when they want to speak to You. There are times when You've kept me safe when I didn't know I was in danger. I'm not some-one who gets in Your way or on Your nerves. You want me to know that I'm worth every moment You spend teaching, correcting, and redirecting me. You make sure I don't run this race alone. Help me get rid of the junk in my life that makes it hard for You to feel welcome. Clean my heart and remove all the baggage. Take what's broken in me and fix it. Remake my life so it looks like the one You knew it could be, Jesus. Amen.

TROUBLE ENDURANCE

*[Jesus said,] "In the world you will
have much trouble. But take hope!
I have power over the world!"*
JOHN 16:33

Trouble! Will it ever end, God? I've seen hard times and tough things. I've seen heartache and broken dreams. I have witnessed sadness and complaint. None of it was a surprise to You. This world has been broken since the very first man and woman broke the only rule You gave them. We've been a mess ever since. People You love break Your rules. And trouble is what happens whenever anyone breaks Your rules. Jesus promised there would be trouble. He was right. But the worst trouble I can imagine is nothing more than an inconvenience for Your power. You can take care of any trouble I face. When You show up, You might bring mercy, love, forgiveness, miracles, or the ability to endure every moment of trouble. Amen.

WHEN TROUBLE SHOWS UP

My Christian brothers, you should be happy when you have all kinds of tests. You know these prove your faith. It helps you not to give up.
JAMES 1:2–3

Giving up looks like I can't take any more, Lord Jesus. It's true. I can't, but You can. You *do*. It seems strange when You say I should be happy when trouble comes. Trouble has never made me happy. But maybe it's the result of trouble that I should be happy about. For instance, trouble teaches me to never give up, to endure, to remember You, and to recognize that You have helped me. Trouble teaches me to look for the good things that happened in the middle of the struggle. The hard times, troubles, and tests are a good way for You to work in my life. You come close to people who feel crushed and brokenhearted. That's why I want to tell You that I think I learn to trust You more when trouble shows up. Amen.

IN THE STRUGGLE

You must be willing to wait without giving up. After you have done what God wants you to do, God will give you what He promised you.
HEBREWS 10:36

Sometimes I face struggles in my life and You, Jesus, require me to endure them because You know that the testing of my faith will make me stronger in the end. This is kind of like a test, and You are checking to see how I'll do. It matters to You that I seek You. It matters to me that I find You. It matters that trouble isn't a forever experience. Thank You for giving me strength when I struggle. Thanks for being my friend when I live through trouble. Thanks for helping me with answers when I face a test. Thanks for giving me a willingness to face trouble with Your help. Before I followed You, I also had trouble, but I didn't have You. There's a big difference between how hard trouble is now that I have You and when I didn't know You. Things are so much better now. Amen.

REJECTING SINFUL THINGS

Turn away from all these sinful things.
Work at being right with God. Live a
God-like life. Have faith and love. Be
willing to wait. Have a kind heart.
1 TIMOTHY 6:11

Sinful things are like an all-you-can-eat restaurant, Jesus—lots to choose from. The difference is that unlike food, sinful things don't satisfy. They look good and want to be noticed. They can't help me to be a better person, son, or friend. They steal the good that You want for me and make me forget the things You've asked me to do. What I should be doing is obeying You, living in a way that shows You're making changes in me, really trusting You, loving others, and being kind to people. These things have all the spiritual nutrition that makes my life like a perfect meal. Keep me coming back to Your table and eating the food that really does satisfy, makes me strong, and helps me endure the test that sinful things bring to me. Help me accept You and reject sin. Amen.

JESUS LEADS, I FOLLOW

*The Lord is my Shepherd. I will
have everything I need.*
PSALM 23:1

You promised something simple so everyone can understand, Lord. You lead Your family, and it's enough. You're the Good Shepherd I follow. Because You're my shepherd and my leader, I don't miss out on anything that matters. You set the schedule, and I can go where You go, and You always go where I go. We're always together. You and I are inseparable. I don't want to see You as someone who interrupts my plans. I want Your plans to be the plans I choose to follow. I want Your rules to make sense to me; when they don't, help me to obey them anyway because Your way is always the right way. Help me trust Your decisions and believe in Your future for me. Amen.

SOMETHING ABOUT
THAT SONG

*"The Lord your God is with you, a Powerful One
Who wins the battle. He will have much joy over
you. With His love He will give you new life.
He will have joy over you with loud singing."*

ZEPHANIAH 3:17

I can hardly believe it, Jesus. I'm flawed and I've failed so many times, but You still think I'm worth a celebration. You fight my battles; You tell me that I bring You joy; You give me new life; You sing a song to me that You wrote. It's like You threw a parade in my honor. The truth is this is what I should be doing for You—well, all but that battle part. I can't do that, but I can try to bring You joy, I can accept Your new life and sing new songs about You. It means a lot to me that I mean so much to You. So today I celebrate You. Amen.

YOU PLANNED AN
AMAZING FUTURE

*" 'I know the plans I have for you,' says
the Lord, 'plans for well-being and not for
trouble, to give you a future and a hope.' "*
JEREMIAH 29:11

Nothing stops Your plans, Jesus. Even when I
can't see what You're doing, You're working for
my best interests. So I want to cooperate with
Your plans and not cause them to go off track.
If I follow You and obey what You ask, then I get
to participate more. I get more responsibility.
If I sit back and wonder if You really know what
You're doing, then I won't get to do as much. So
I need to trust You and take part in Your plans.
The Bible says Your plans are for my safety and
won't cause me more trouble than I already
face. I trust that Your plans are good, and even
if it takes awhile to work them out, I'll see an
amazing future. Thank You. Amen.

THE GOOD RULES

*The Laws of the Lord are right, giving
joy to the heart. The Word of the Lord
is pure, giving light to the eyes.*
PSALM 19:8

It matters to You that Your commands bring joy,
Lord Jesus. These rules are good because they
show that You want everything I do to connect
with Your law of love. It's amazing to see how
people respond to kindness and love. People
will always do big things for people they love.
It's harder to want to help people who make
others afraid. I might do what a bully says, but
I don't really want to—and I'll even wish I hadn't
listened to them. But I'll care for others because
You asked and because I love You. No one can
make rules that are better, because Your laws
make everyone welcome and ask that people always choose love. Who thinks that's a bad idea?
Amen.

PRAYING AS MUCH AS I WANT

*You must keep praying. Keep
watching! Be thankful always.*
COLOSSIANS 4:2

I say words to You that mean something to me, Jesus. It's called prayer, and You want to hear from me. I don't need to stop praying either. I might be interrupted by school or supper, but I can pray to You whenever I have a little time—and it's time that is never wasted. You hear what I have to say, and I get to know You better. It can bring praise to a mouth that has not always been used to saying, "Thank You!" Praying to You is so much better than keeping my thoughts to myself. Whatever concerns me is important to You too. That may be why You want me to pray as much as I want. Amen.

READ TO LISTEN

God's Word is living and powerful. It is sharper than a sword that cuts both ways. It cuts straight into where the soul and spirit meet and it divides them. It cuts into the joints and bones. It tells what the heart is thinking about and what it wants to do.

Hebrews 4:12

The Bible knows who I am, Jesus. It talks about being selfish—I've been selfish. It talks about forgiving others—there are times I don't want to. It talks about love—I need to do more of that. It's a powerful book. The Bible shows what's wrong with me and what's right with You. It guides me to good places. It puts up stop signs to places I shouldn't visit. It helps me see who I really am and then shows me what I can be. The Bible shows me the best way to get to where I need to go and can redirect me if I get off track. It's where You speak to me and where I listen to You. Amen.

THE FOUR QUESTIONS

Are you strong because you belong to Christ?
Does His love comfort you? Do you have joy
by being as one in sharing the Holy Spirit?
Do you have loving-kindness and pity for each
other? Then give me true joy by thinking
the same thoughts. Keep having the same
love. Be as one in thoughts and actions.
PHILIPPIANS 2:1–2

I can say yes to the four questions in this scripture passage, Lord Jesus. You make me strong. I'm comforted by You. Your Spirit makes me joyful. And I'm learning to love others and show them kindness. Since there are others around me who would also say yes to these four questions, then please help us work together to do even more. We're doing the same work and we're doing this work for You. Unity is Your good idea, and it matters to You. You don't want Christians to leave other Christians out of the good things You're doing. Help me include other members of Your family when I follow Your good plan. Amen.

WHAT NO ONE ELSE COULD DO

You must be kind to each other. Think of the other person. Forgive other people just as God forgave you because of Christ's death on the cross.

Ephesians 4:32

When others break Your rules and I get hurt, Jesus, give me the willingness to forgive them. Because forgiving others can be hard, I might not be able to do it without Your help. Remind me of how You forgave me and then gave me the Holy Spirit so that I have the power to forgive people who hurt me. I can learn from You. It was Your kindness that made me a friend in the first place. When You forgave me, I came to understand that You were doing something for me that no one else had done or even could do. So I can take what You've done and do the same thing for others as a way to let You know that I'm grateful for all You've done, are doing, and will do for me. Amen.

BE FAIR, BE KIND, BE HUMBLE

O man, He has told you what is good.
What does the Lord ask of you but to do
what is fair and to love kindness, and to
walk without pride with your God?
MICAH 6:8

You share good things, Jesus. I hear bad news almost everywhere I go, but that's never been true of You. Well, that's not entirely true. You did say that I broke Your rules, and that wasn't good news. Then You had a rescue plan for that. And that was really great news. Something You ask me to do sounds simple but is harder than it sounds. You ask me to be fair, be kind, and be humble. I should be able to do that, but I can't do it in my own power. I'm not always fair. Sometimes I'm rude. Pride shows up when I don't want it. I know it's important to You that I'm fair, kind, and humble, so please help me by the power of the Holy Spirit inside me. Thank You! Amen.

WHEN I'M NOT SO SURE

*"No one can have greater love than
to give his life for his friends."*
JOHN 15:13

The thing that matters more than anything is You, Lord Jesus. You made a way for me to be made right with You. Without You, there would be no forever way to be friends with You. It was love that allowed You to lay down Your life for friends like me. You are perfect, but I'm not. You easily forgive while I wait to forgive. You love even when I'm not so sure. It would be nice to make the right choices every time I have a choice to make, but only You can do that. You made the choice to love imperfect people and make a way for us to be friends. Since I matter to You, let me choose every day to let You know that You matter to me. Let me follow when it's hard, obey when I have questions, and ask for help when I struggle. Amen.

SCRIPTURE INDEX

OLD TESTAMENT